GUY TAPLIN

2015

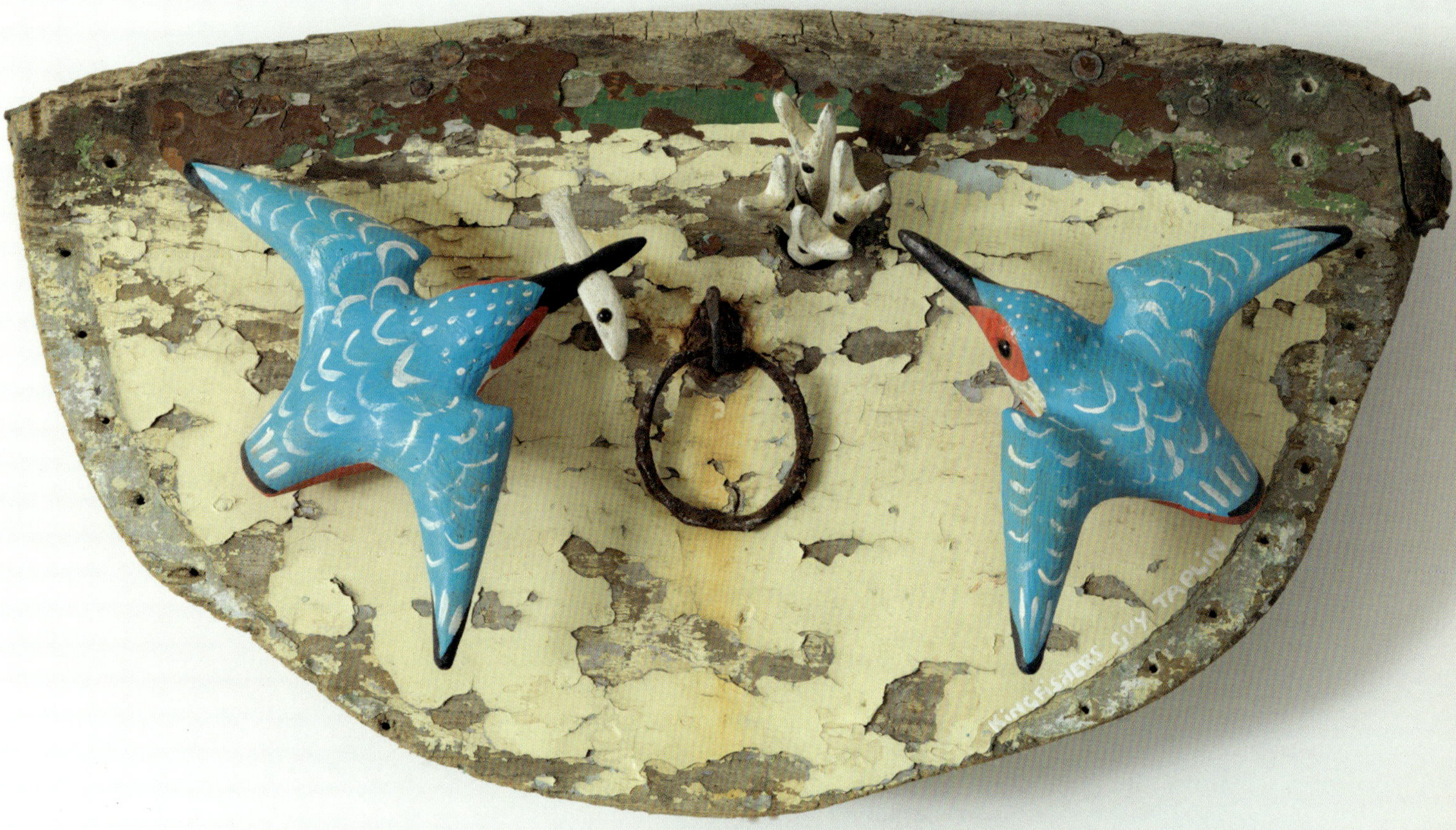

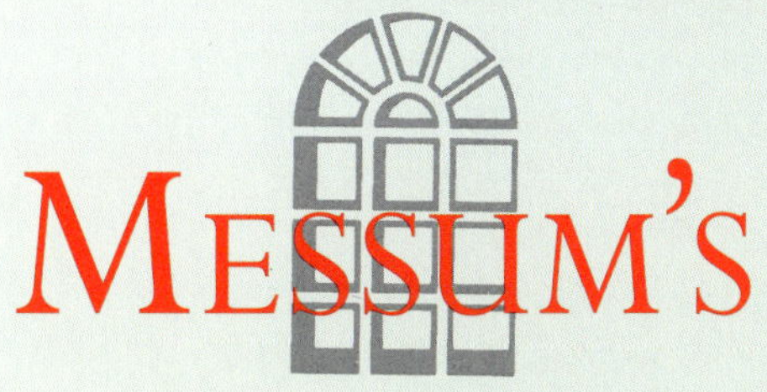

www.messums.com

28 Cork Street, London W1S 3NG
Telephone: +44 (0)20 7437 5545

Foreword

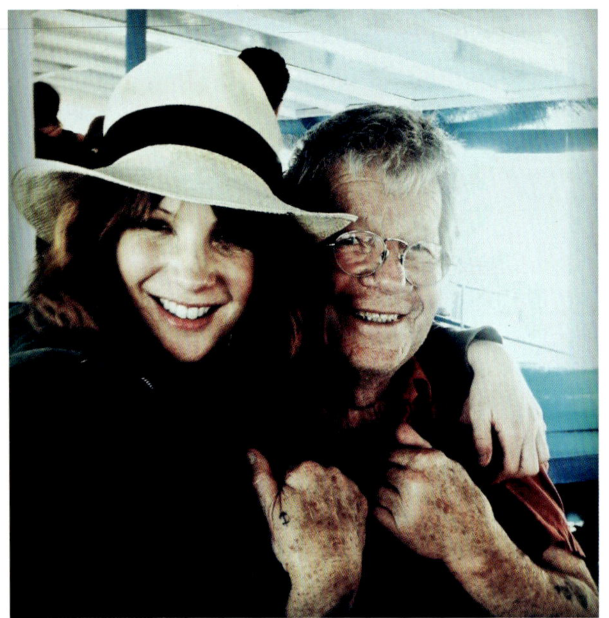

Nancy and Guy Taplin

In our downstairs bathroom, on the wall opposite a large, weather-beaten crucifix, there's a small shelf. Propped at the back, amidst the usual bathroom detritus – discarded toothbrushes, nail clippers and huge iridescent shells – is a small, framed picture. The frame is old, and the image it holds is faded and water-stained. If you were to prise the back off, you'd find a photo long ago cut from a book.

Even were it less time-bleached, the picture would still be stark in its simplicity. A sparse landscape, empty of people, unfolds into the middle distance. Several stands of Marram grass grow amidst gently sloping sand dunes, and behind them you can just catch a glimpse of the sea…

In a house that's crammed with all manner of eye-catching curios – from tribal masks to narwhal tusks – it might seem strange to single out such an apparently unprepossessing object. But in some ways, this is the most important object of all; it's a touchstone to the story of my father's life and to the beautiful mythology that he's woven into the fabric of my own.

Looking at the photo is like lifting a shell to your ear; it whispers a promise. I can imagine my father – still only a child – encountering the picture for the first time, his eyes seeking a path through the sand dunes, his ears hearing the sea's prescient murmur as his scissors cut into the page.

He may not have realized it at the time, but this was my father finding his habitat. Like the birds he's spent his life sculpting, he's most at home in these wild empty quarters. That's why my brother and I spent so much of our childhoods as salty-haired sea urchins, and grew up expertly trained in the arts of beachcombing and rolling around in the mud.

One of my favourite images of Dad is a black and white photo that Mum keeps on her dresser. In it, he strides down a sloping shingle beach, hunkered slightly into the weight of the long plank of timber that's perfectly balanced upon the straight of his shoulder.

This is an archetypal 'Dad pose'. He's in his seventies now, but still I pass a good portion of each summer tracing his uneven footsteps as he and his knee replacement haul improbably large bits of driftwood along the deserted Portuguese coast.

In the local bars there, they call him "the beach cleaner". The Portuguese are naturally reticent, but I suspect we've become eccentric fixtures in their summer calendars, drawn there every year as surely as the myriad migratory birds.

And so we spend the warm months moving to and fro across the barrier islands, their fragile, paired-down landscapes being forever reshaped by the whims of weather and tide. We've built up ritual through repetition, establishing sacred resting points beneath the arches of an abandoned army base and the sibilant branches of a solitary tree.

Every day is a new odyssey, spent seeking out the bleached bones of old boats, long marooned up transient tidal inlets. Journeying back to the town, we stand at the bows of a battle-weary armada of ferries, watching sanderlings flit purposefully across the shipping path in groups of twos and threes.

Just as this marshy seaboard is a rich feeding ground for shorebirds, flamingos, storks and spoonbills, so too it provides my father with a seemingly endless supply of creative and spiritual sustenance. It's here that his sculptures are born, taking shape in his mind whilst we wander this skeleton coast of the soul.

Nancy Taplin

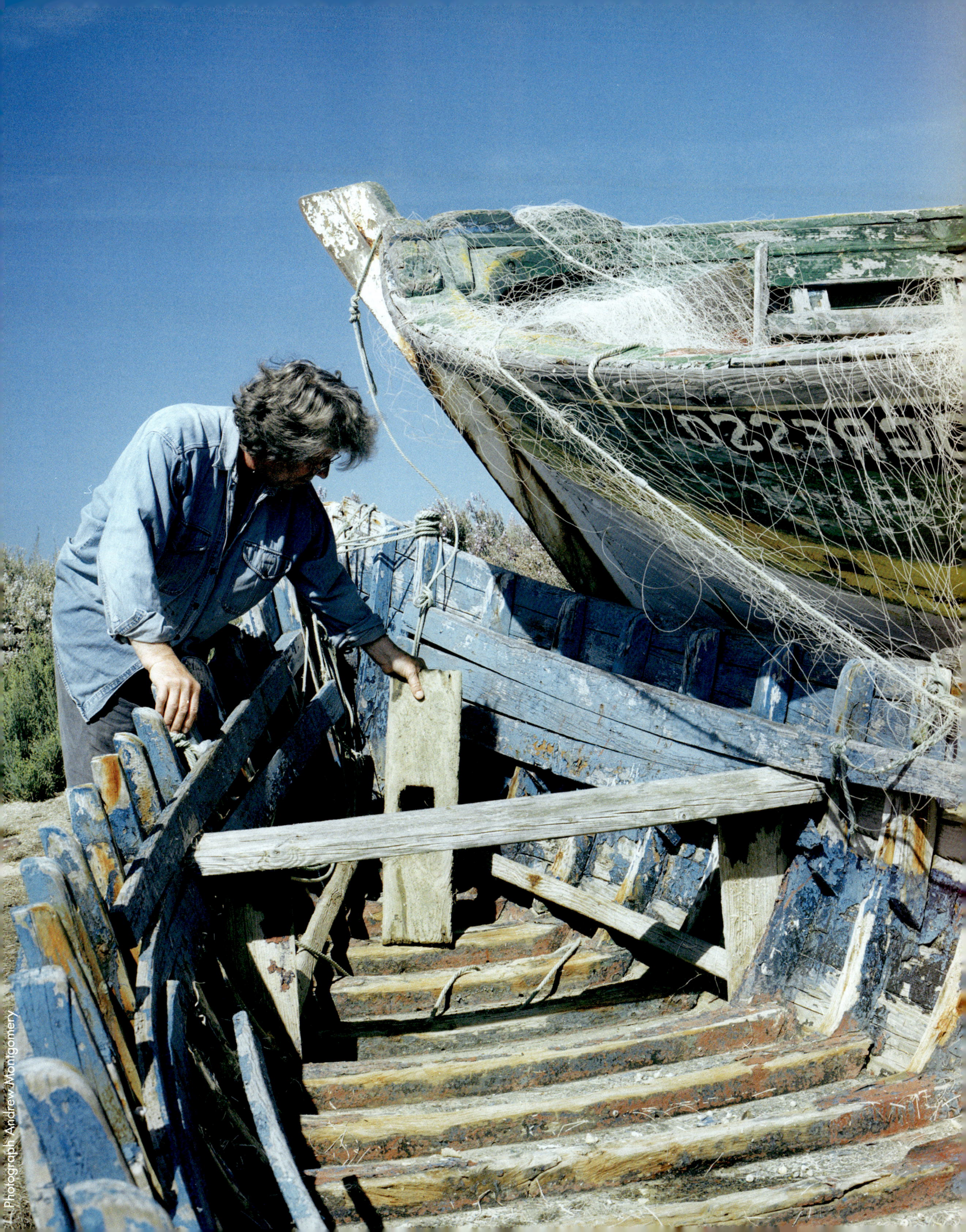

Photograph: Andrew Montgomery

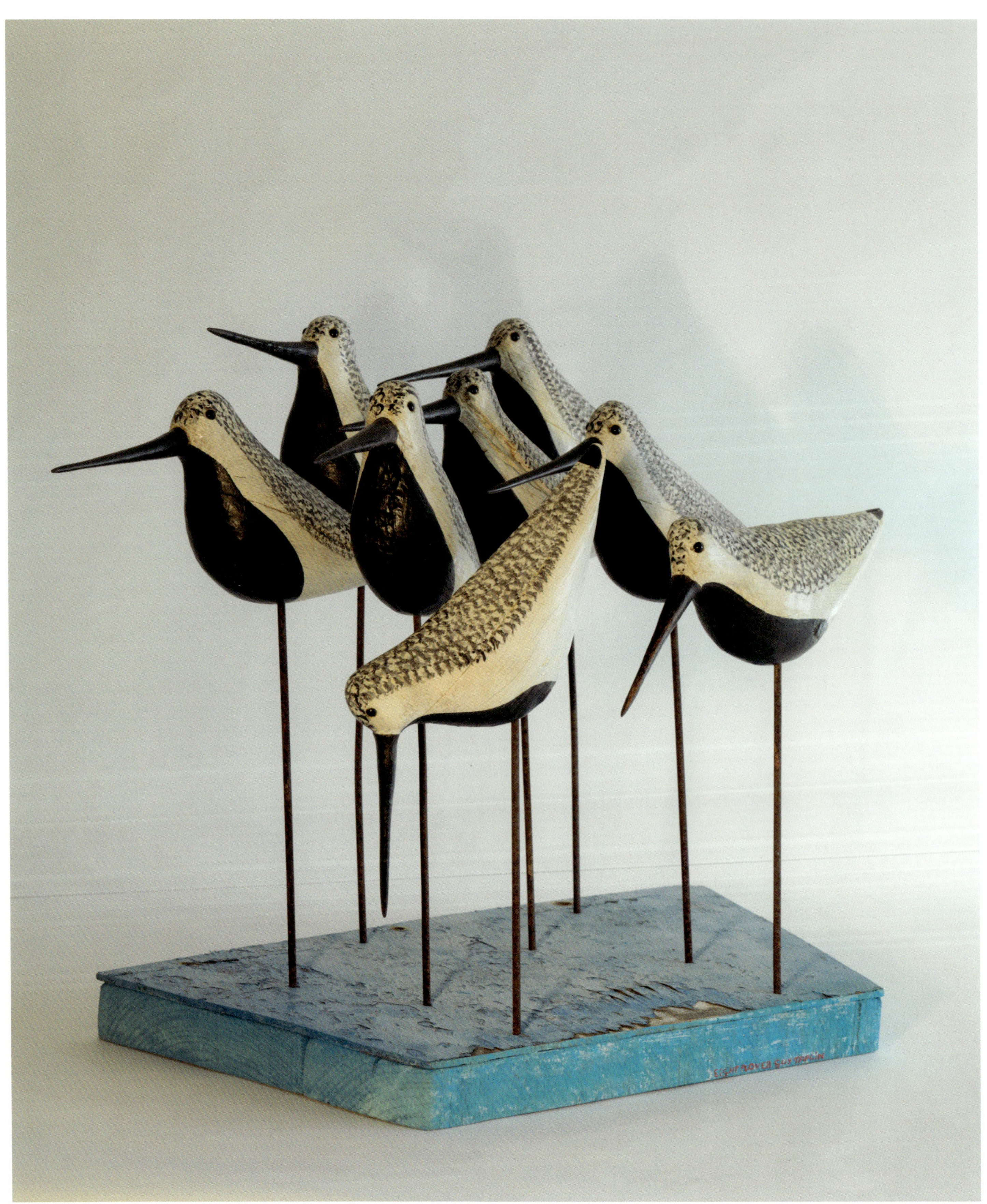

3. **Eight Plover**
carved and painted driftwood
56 x 66 x 38 cms   22 x 25¾ x 15 ins

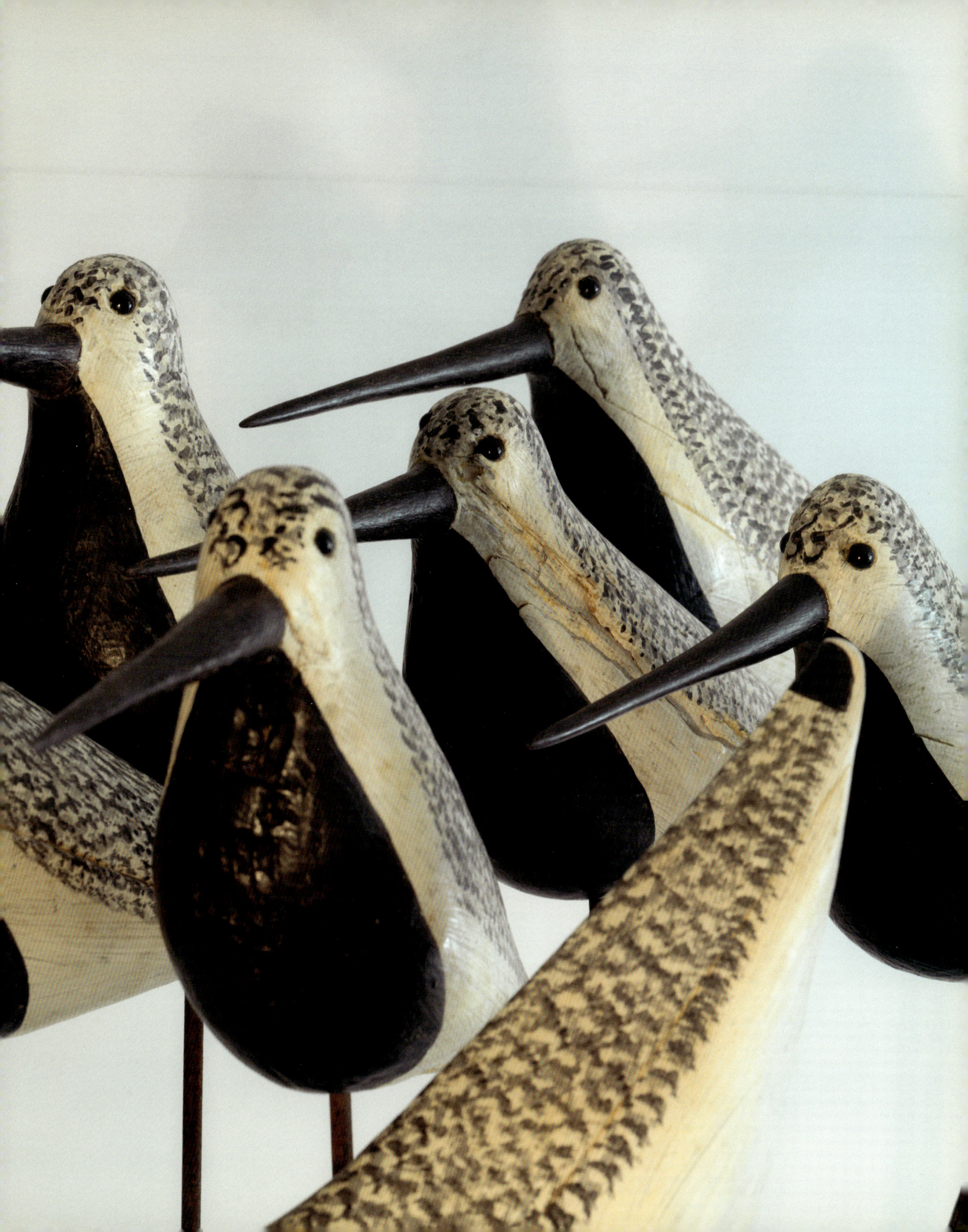

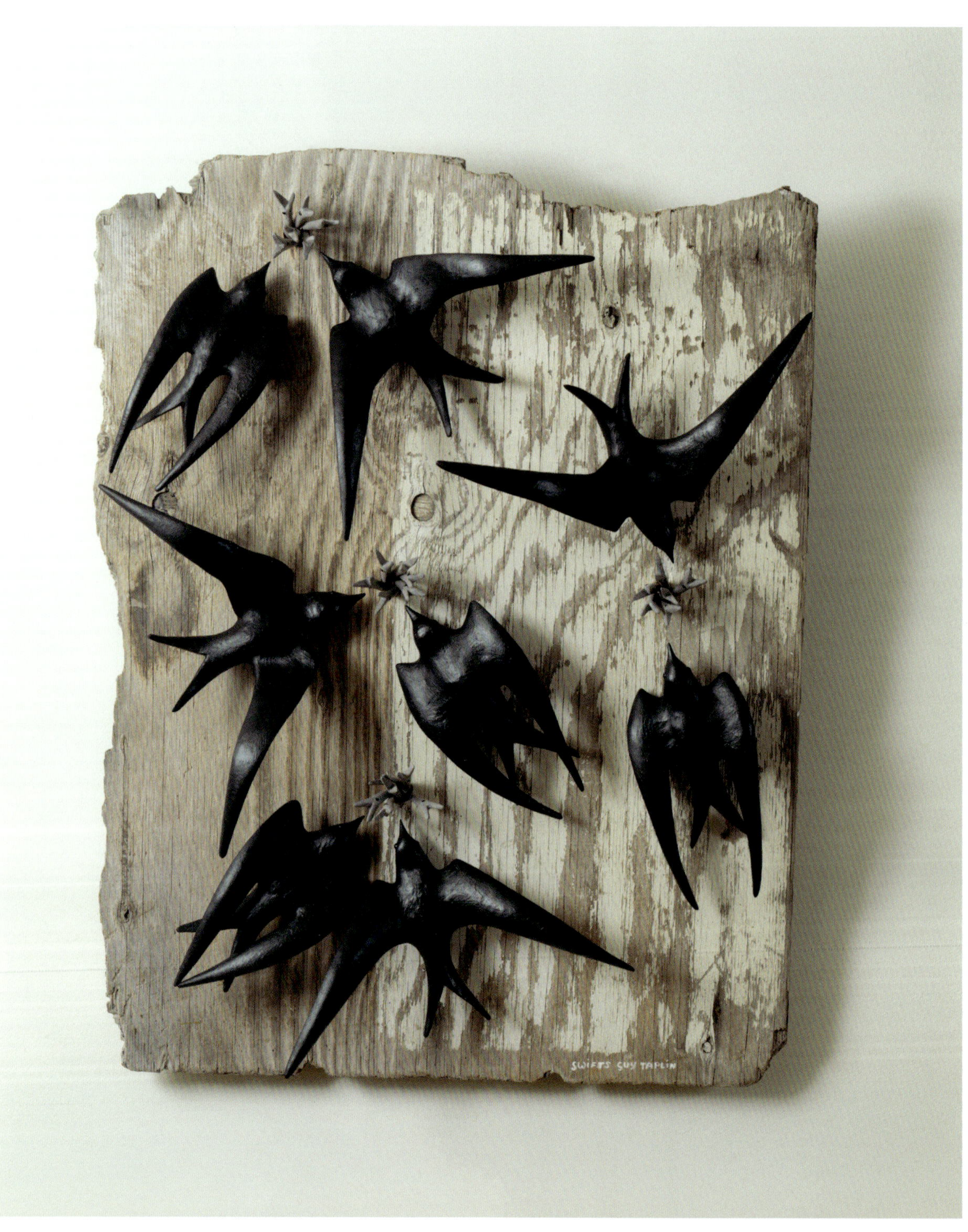

4. **SWIFTS ON A PANEL**
carved and painted driftwood
81 x 65 x 18 cms   31⅞ x 25⅝ x 7⅛ ins

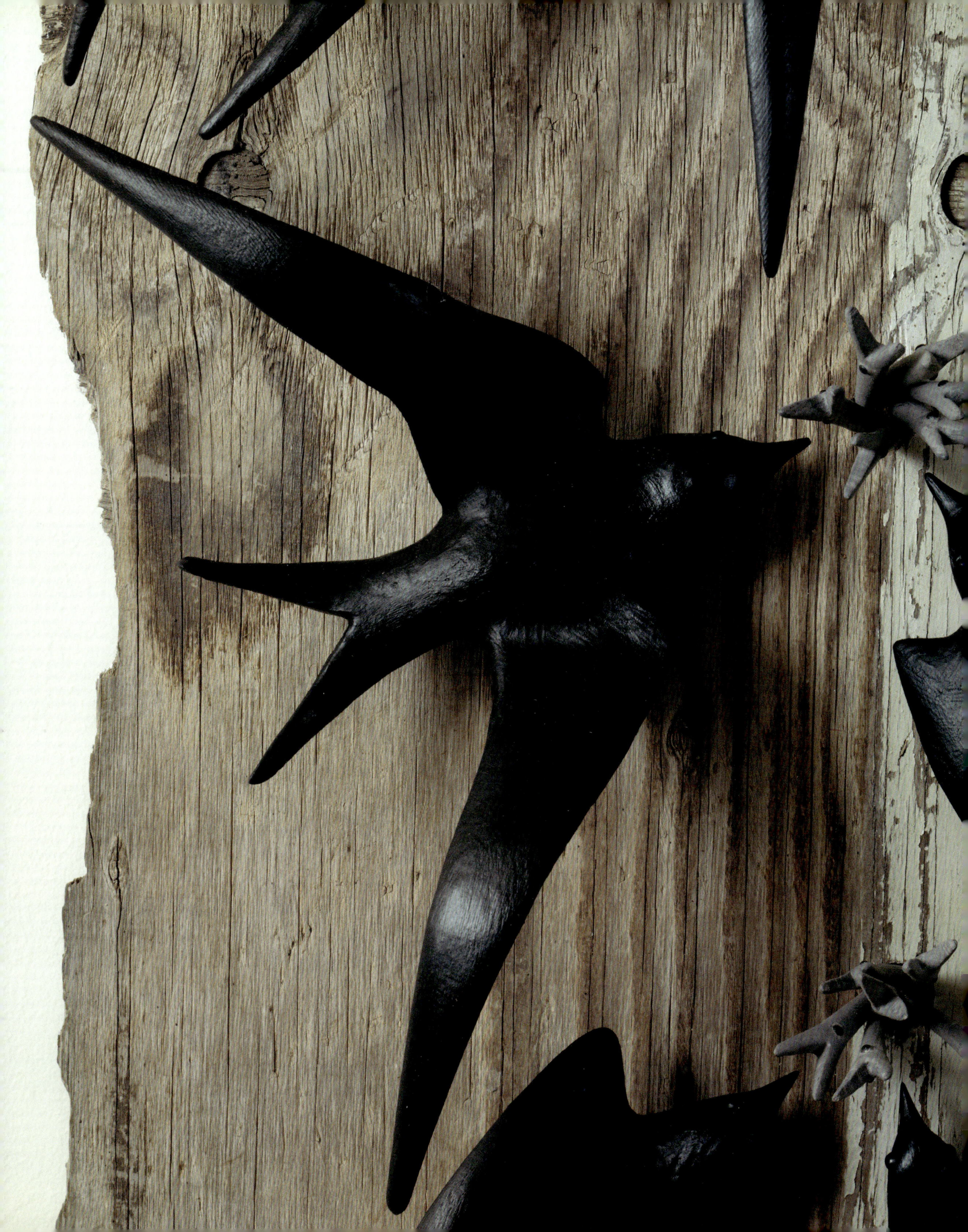

5. TEN SPOONBILL

carved and painted driftwood

110 x 109 x 85 cms $43\frac{1}{4}$ x $42\frac{7}{8}$ x $33\frac{1}{2}$ ins

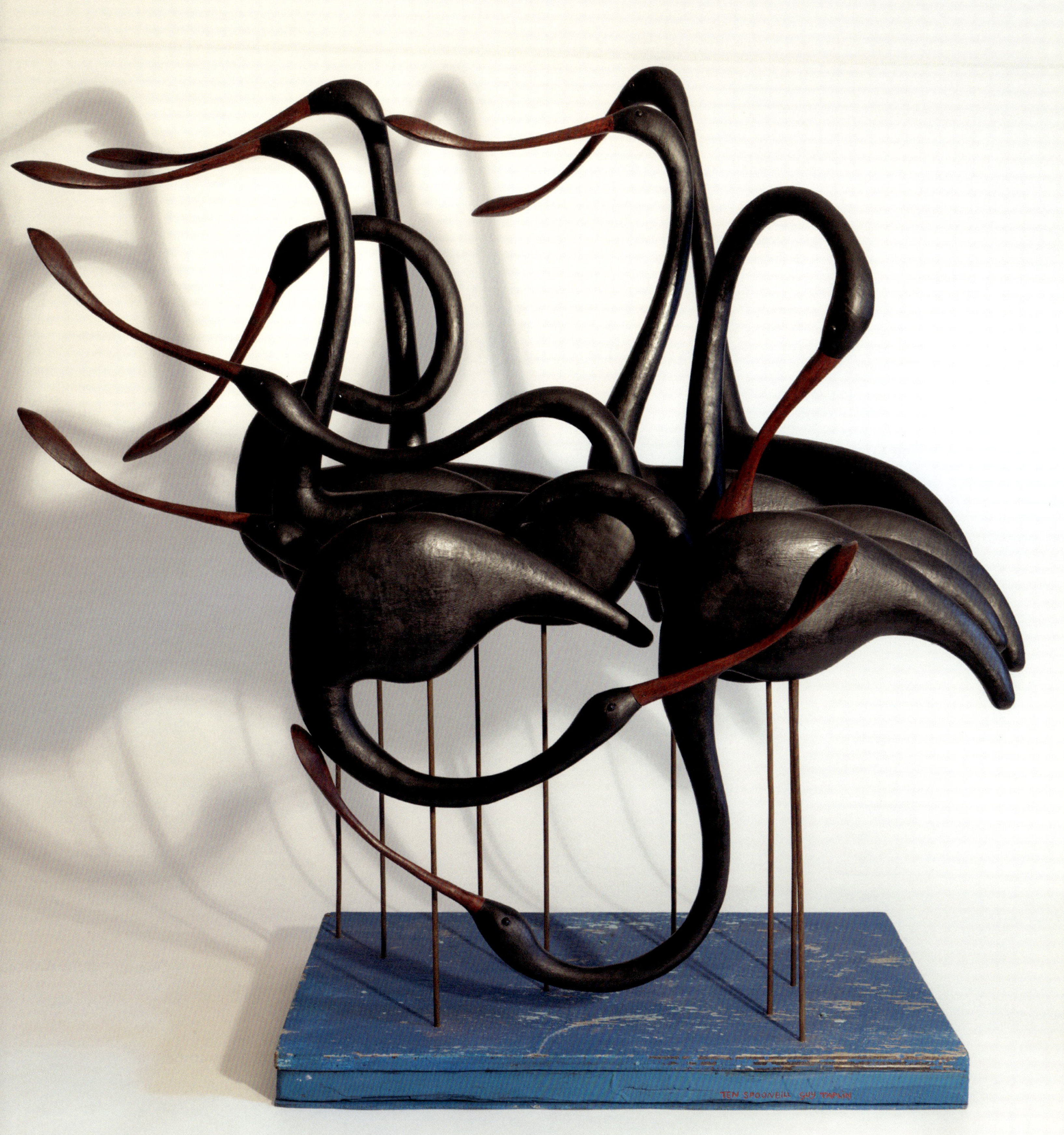
TEN SPOONBILL GUY TAPLIN

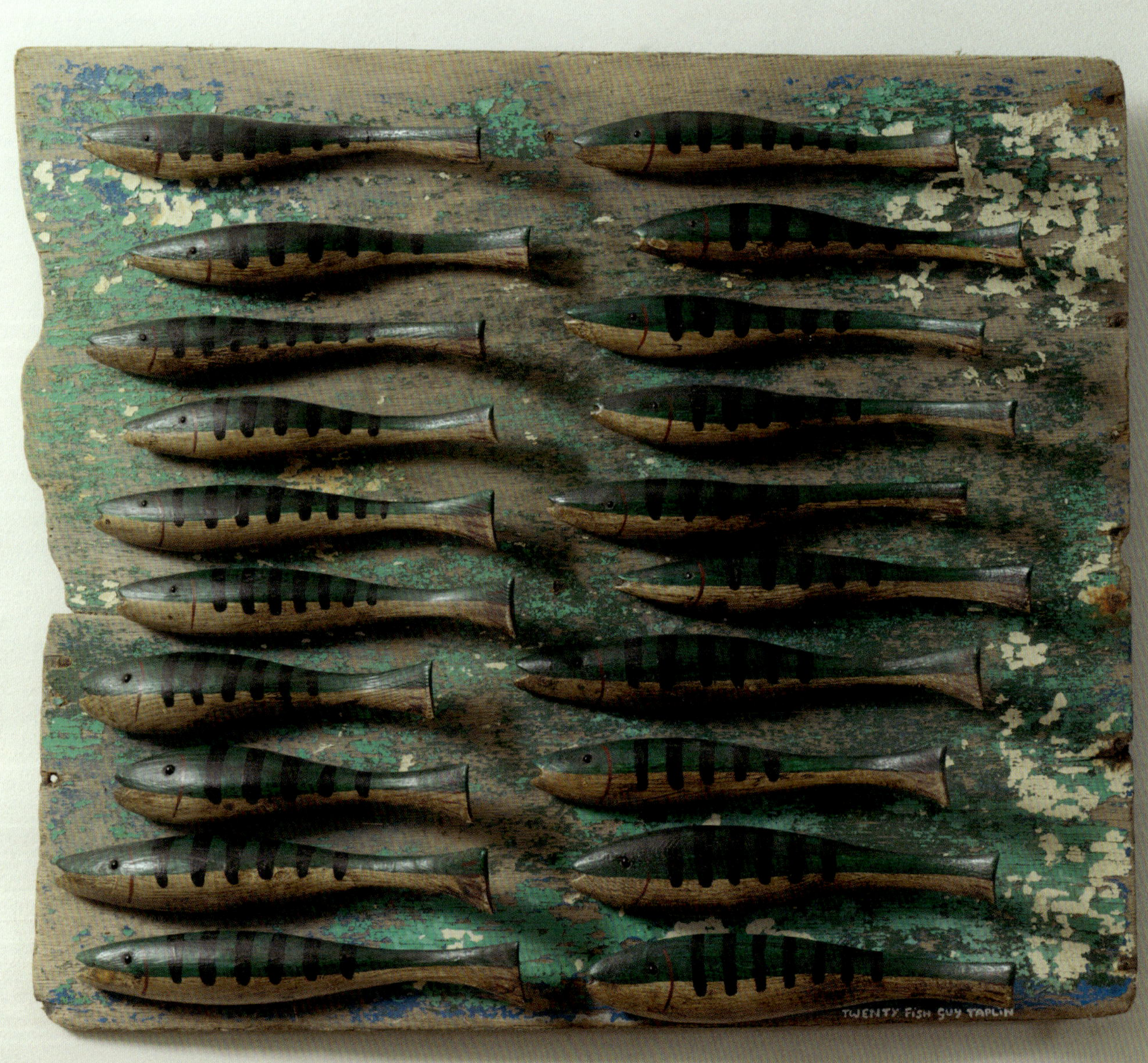

6. TWENTY FISH
carved and painted driftwood
54 x 64 x 11 cms 21¼ x 25 x 4⅜ ins

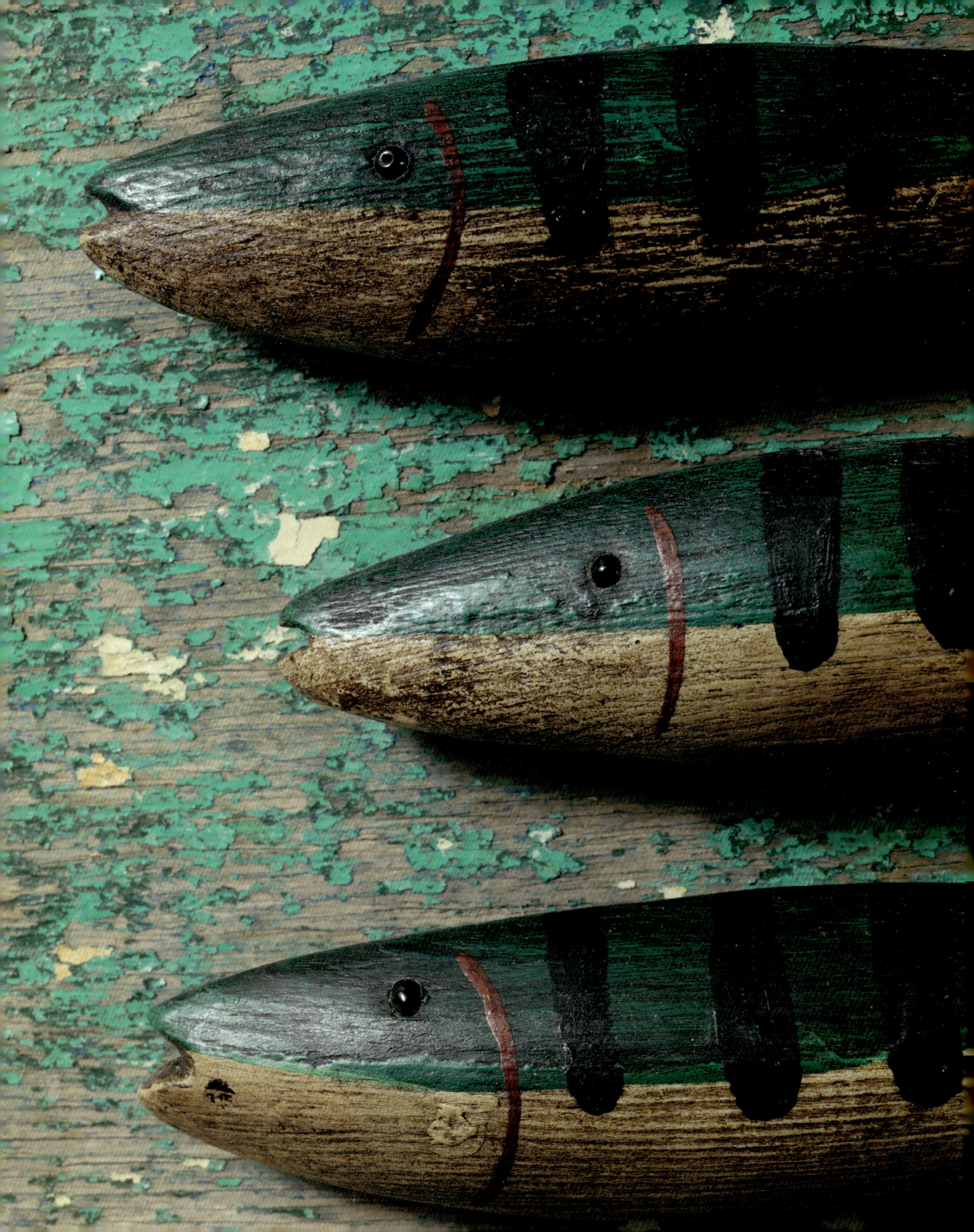

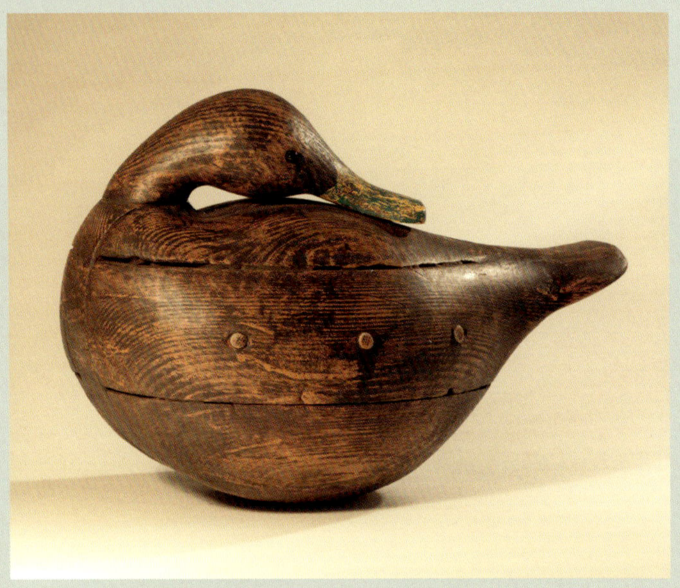

7. **Duck**
carved and painted driftwood
25 x 38 x 24 cms   9⅞ x 15 x 9½ ins

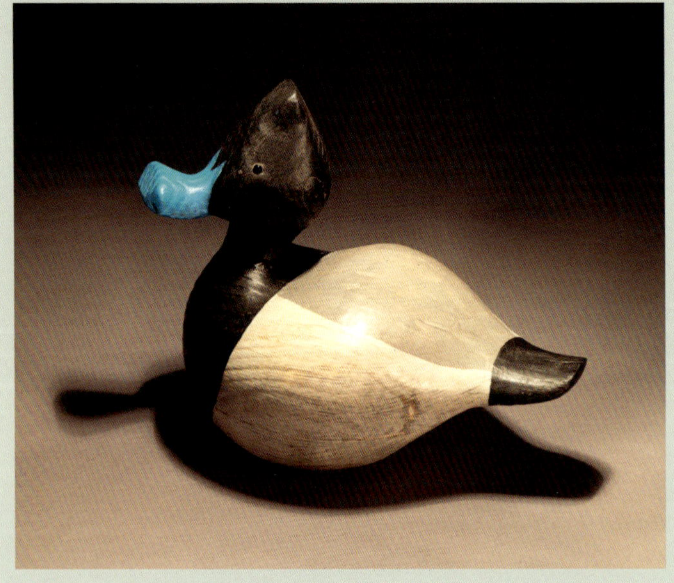

8. **Small Scaup**
carved and painted driftwood
21 x 28 x 18 cms   8¼ x 10⅞ x 6⅞ ins

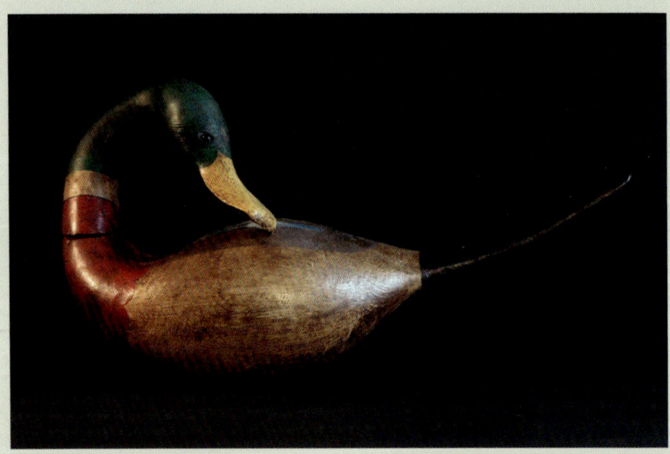

9. **Preening Mallard**
carved and painted driftwood
25 x 51 x 20 cms   9⅞ x 20⅛ x 7⅞ ins

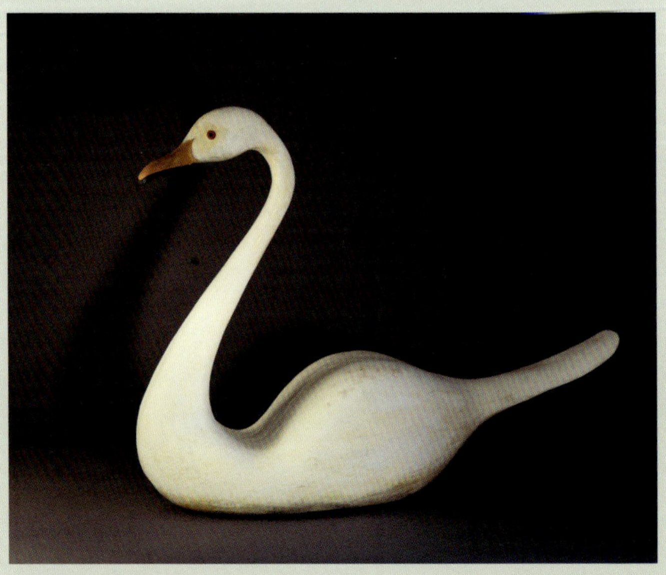

10. **Swan** (detail opposite)
carved and painted driftwood
79 x 106 x 35 cms   31⅛ x 41¾ x 13¾ ins

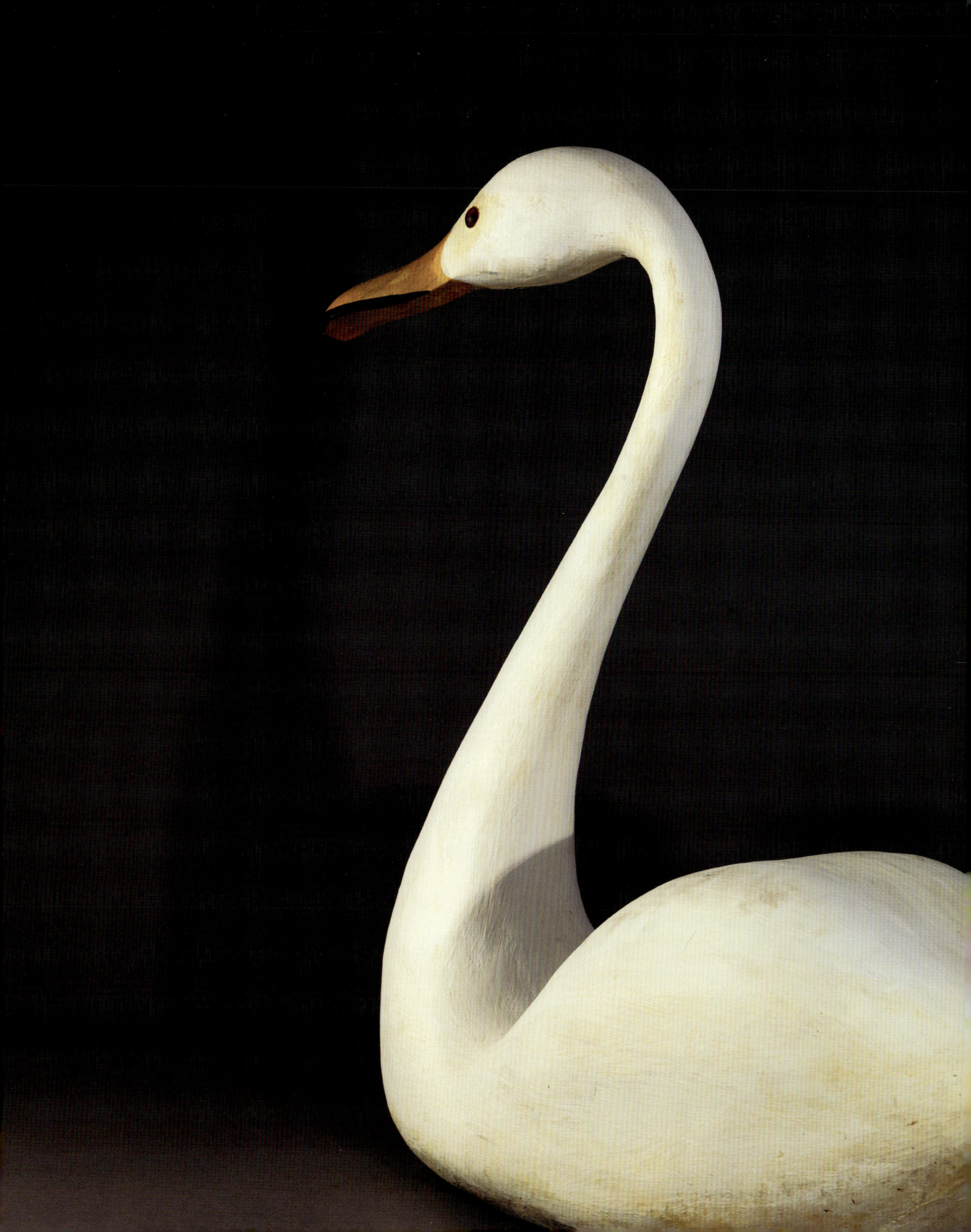

11. **Peep**
carved and painted driftwood
23 x 14 x 8 cms 8⅞ x 5⅜ x 3⅛ ins

12. **Plover**
carved and painted driftwood
35 x 21 x 11 cms 13¾ x 8¼ x 4⅛ ins

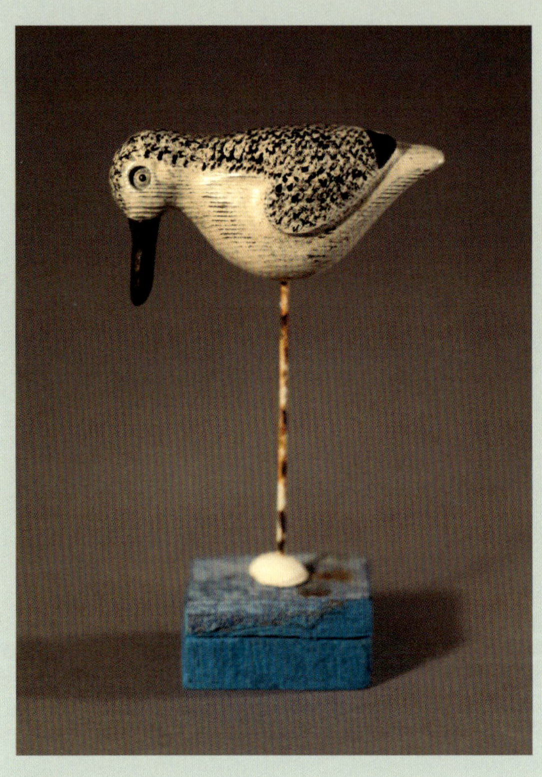

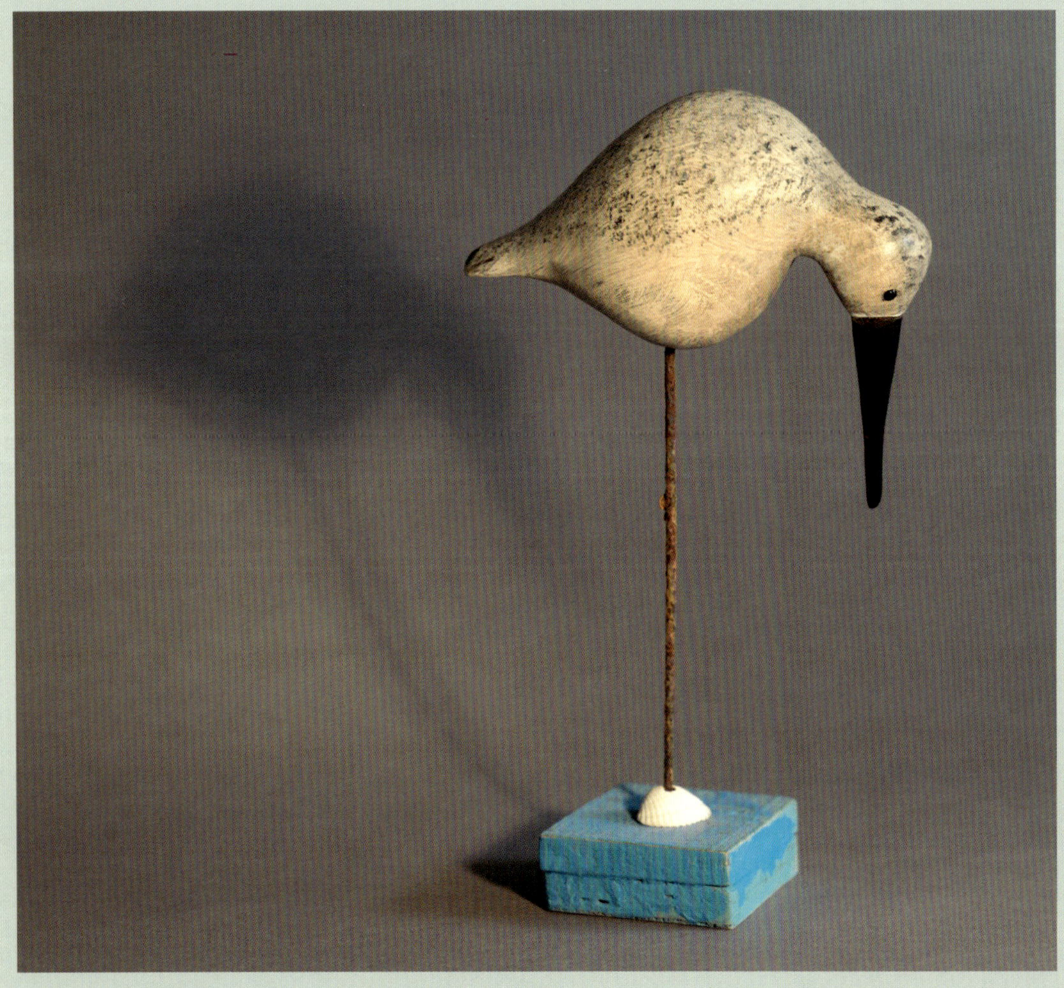

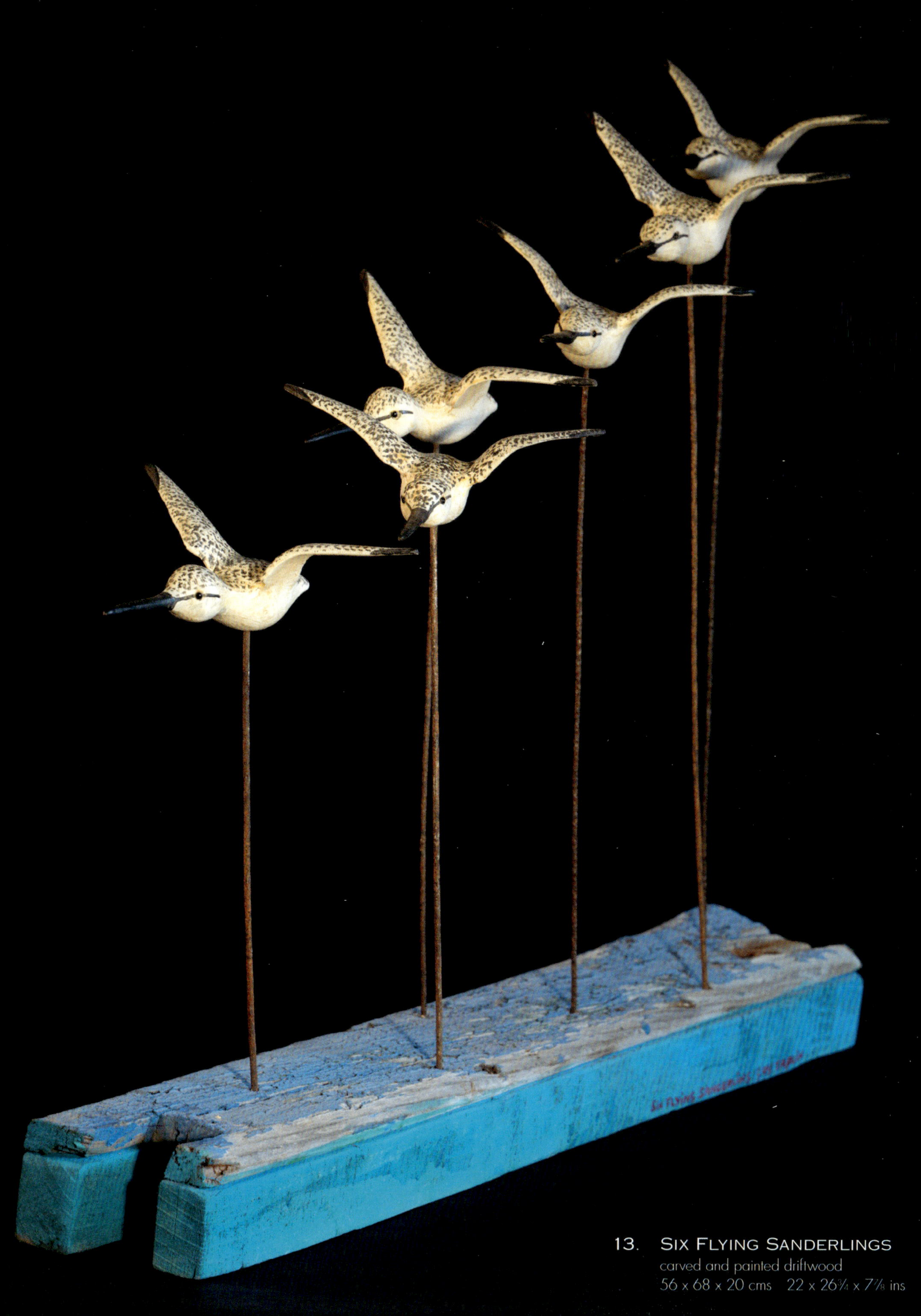

13. Six Flying Sanderlings
carved and painted driftwood
56 x 68 x 20 cms 22 x 26¾ x 7⅞ ins

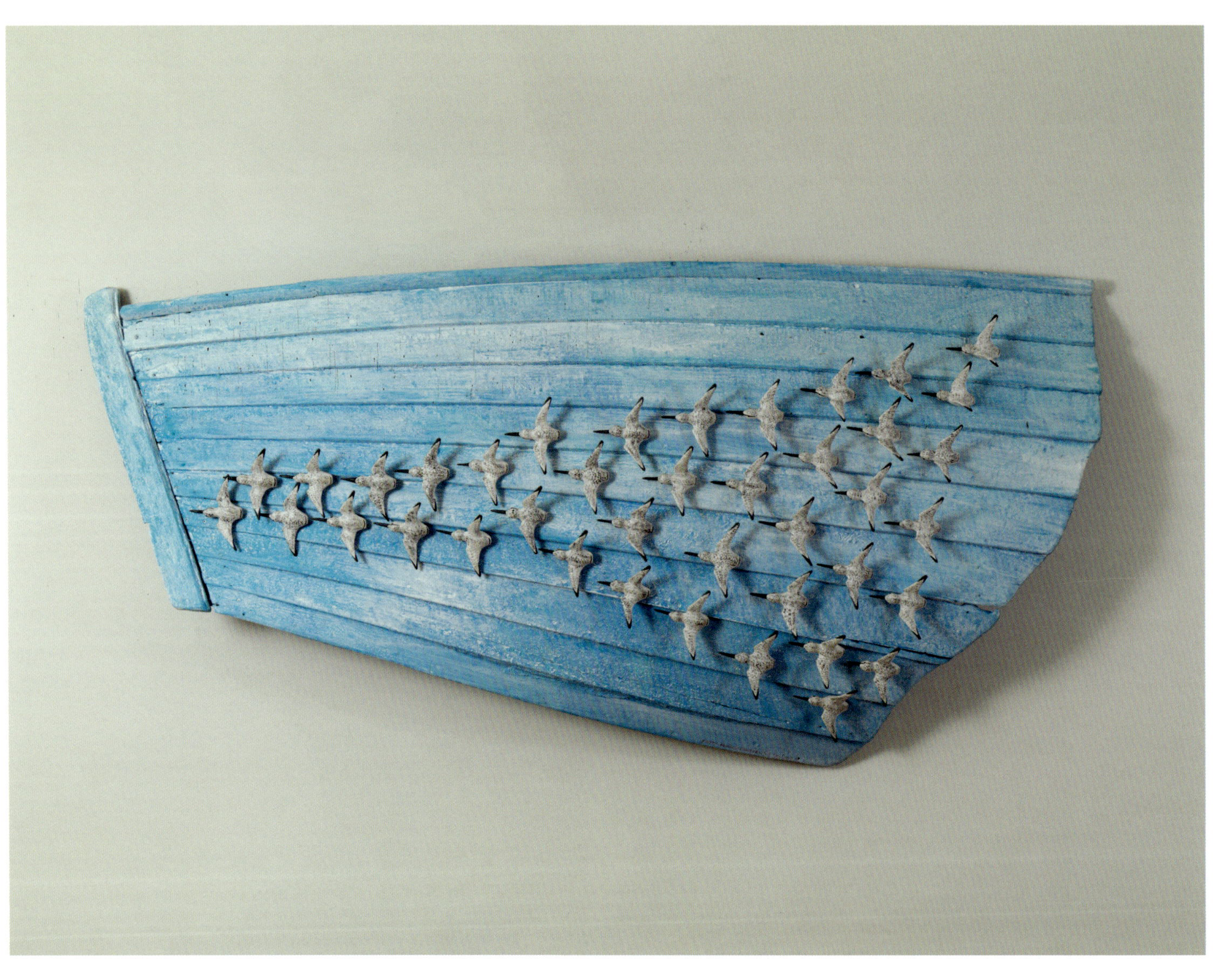

14. **Forty Flying Sanderlings on a Boat Panel**
carved and painted driftwood
91 x 173 x 26 cms   35⅞ x 68⅛ x 10¼ ins

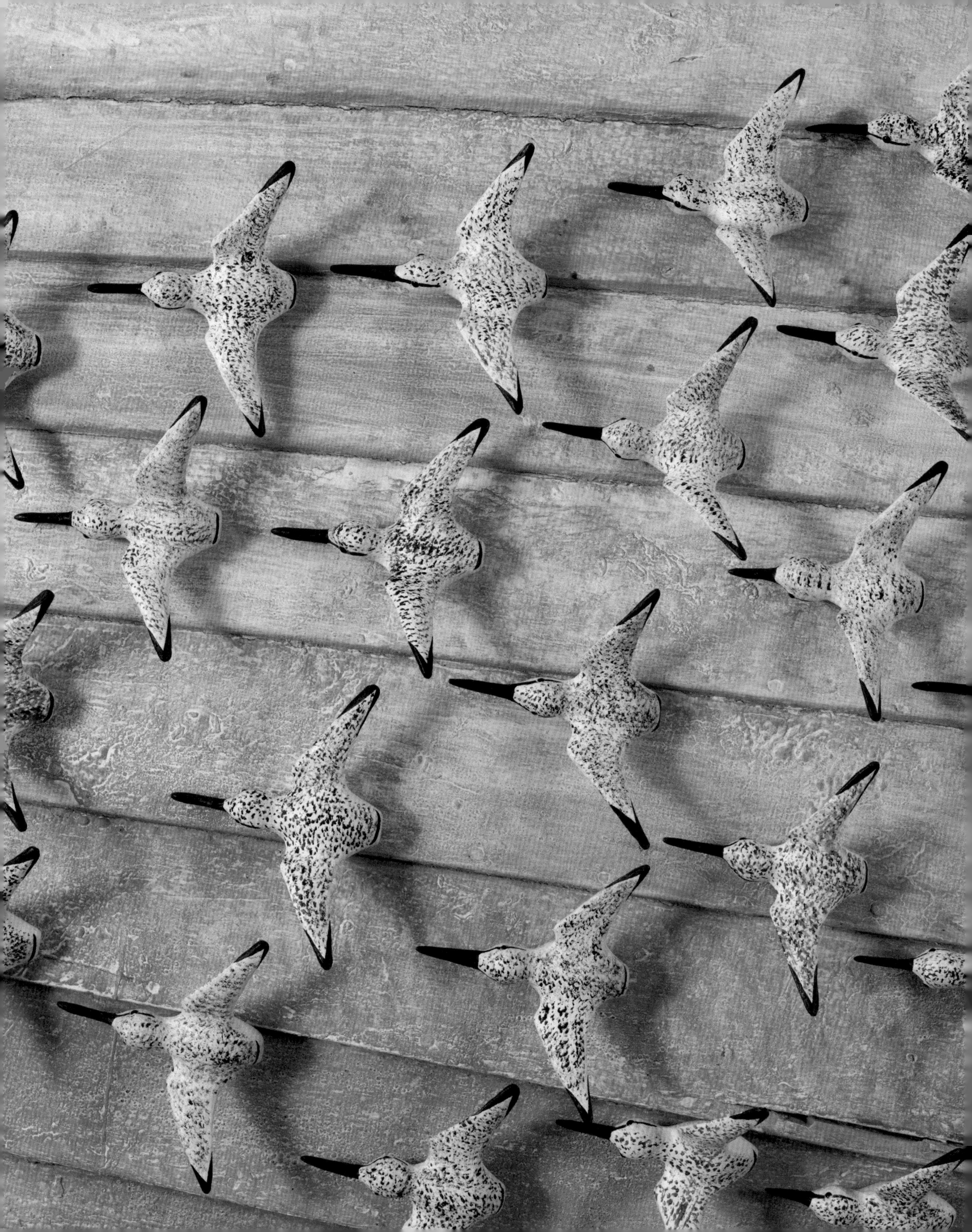

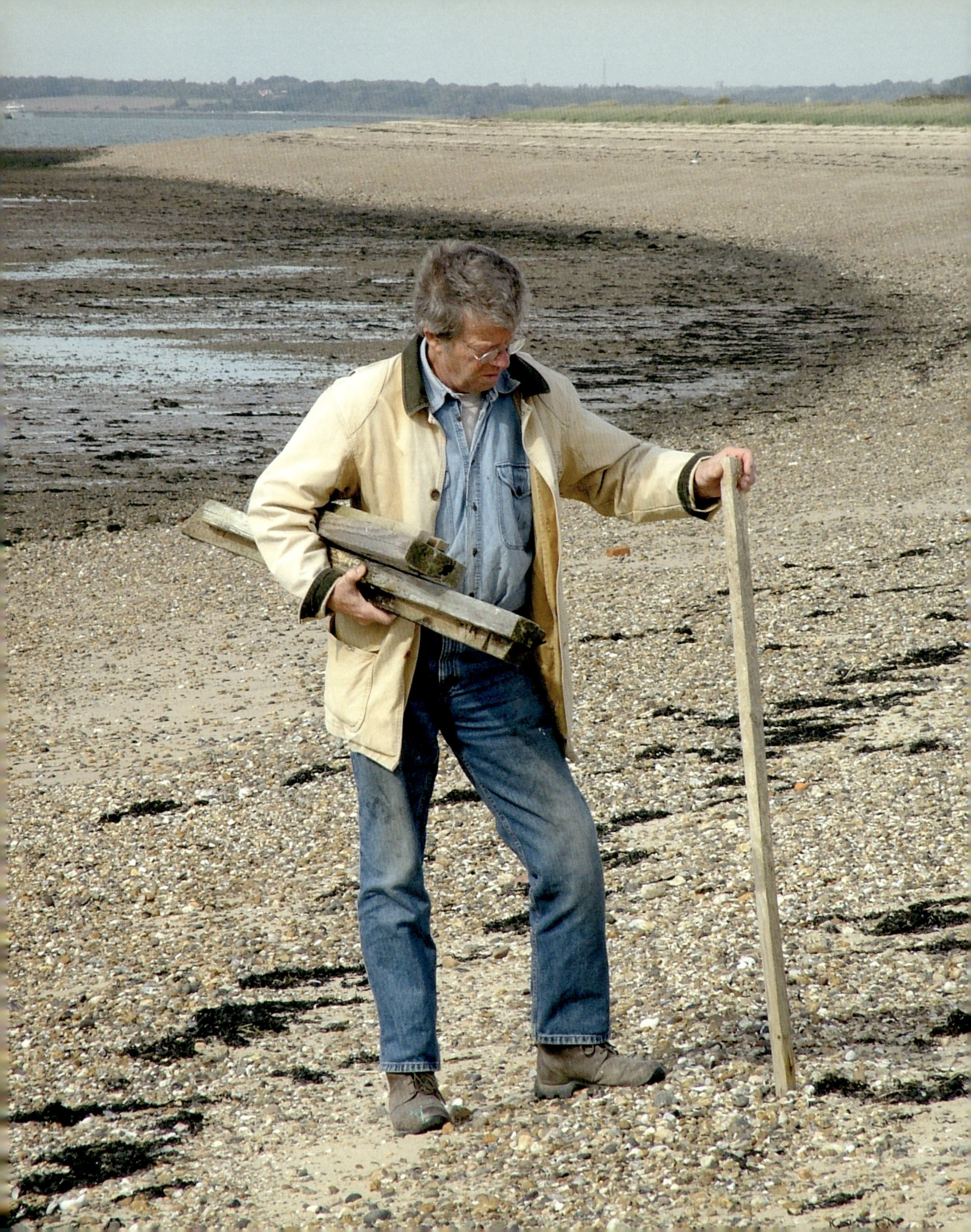

15. EIGHT SHOREBIRDS
carved and painted driftwood
68 x 68 x 31 cms 26¾ x 26¾ x 12¼ ins

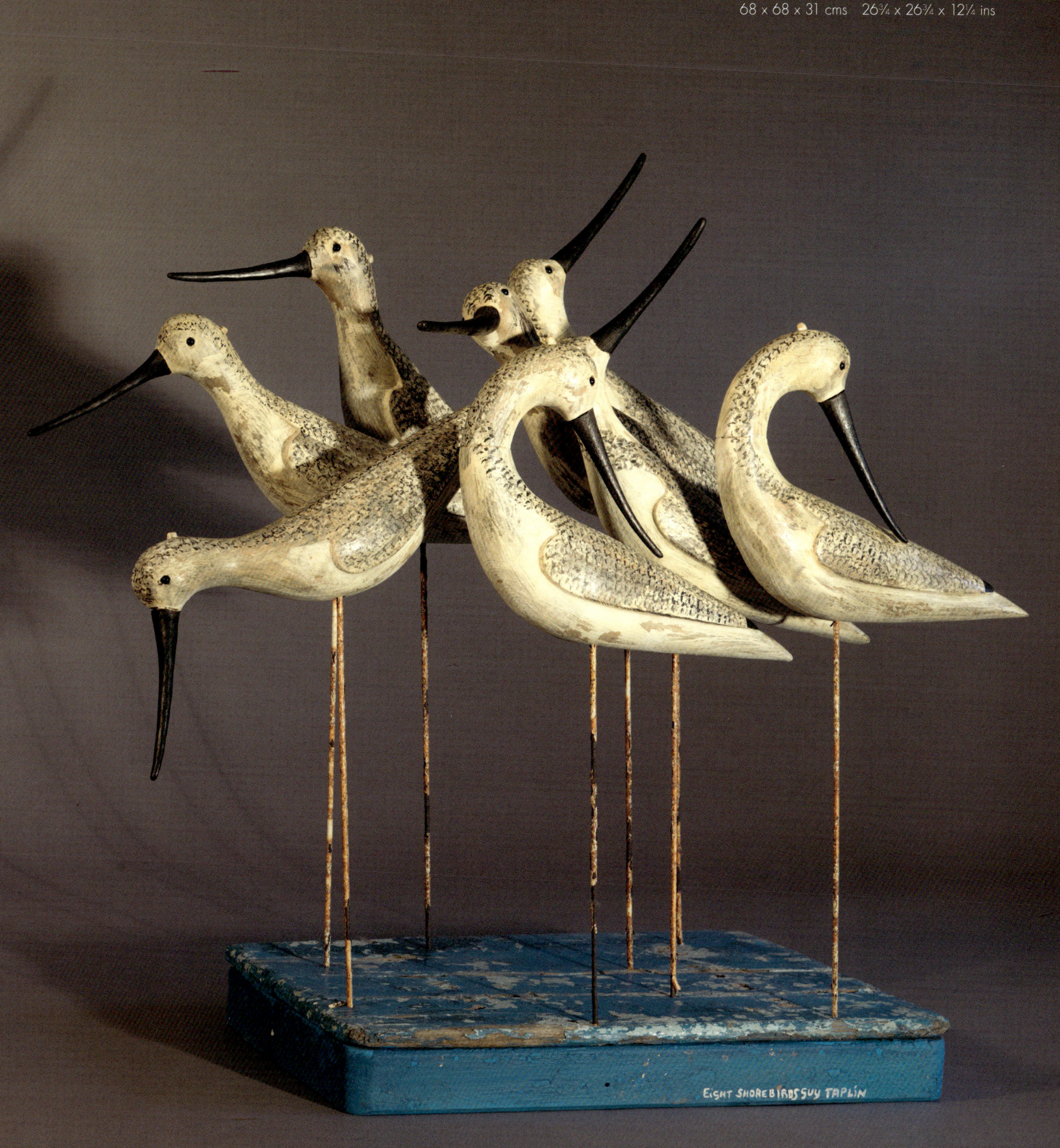

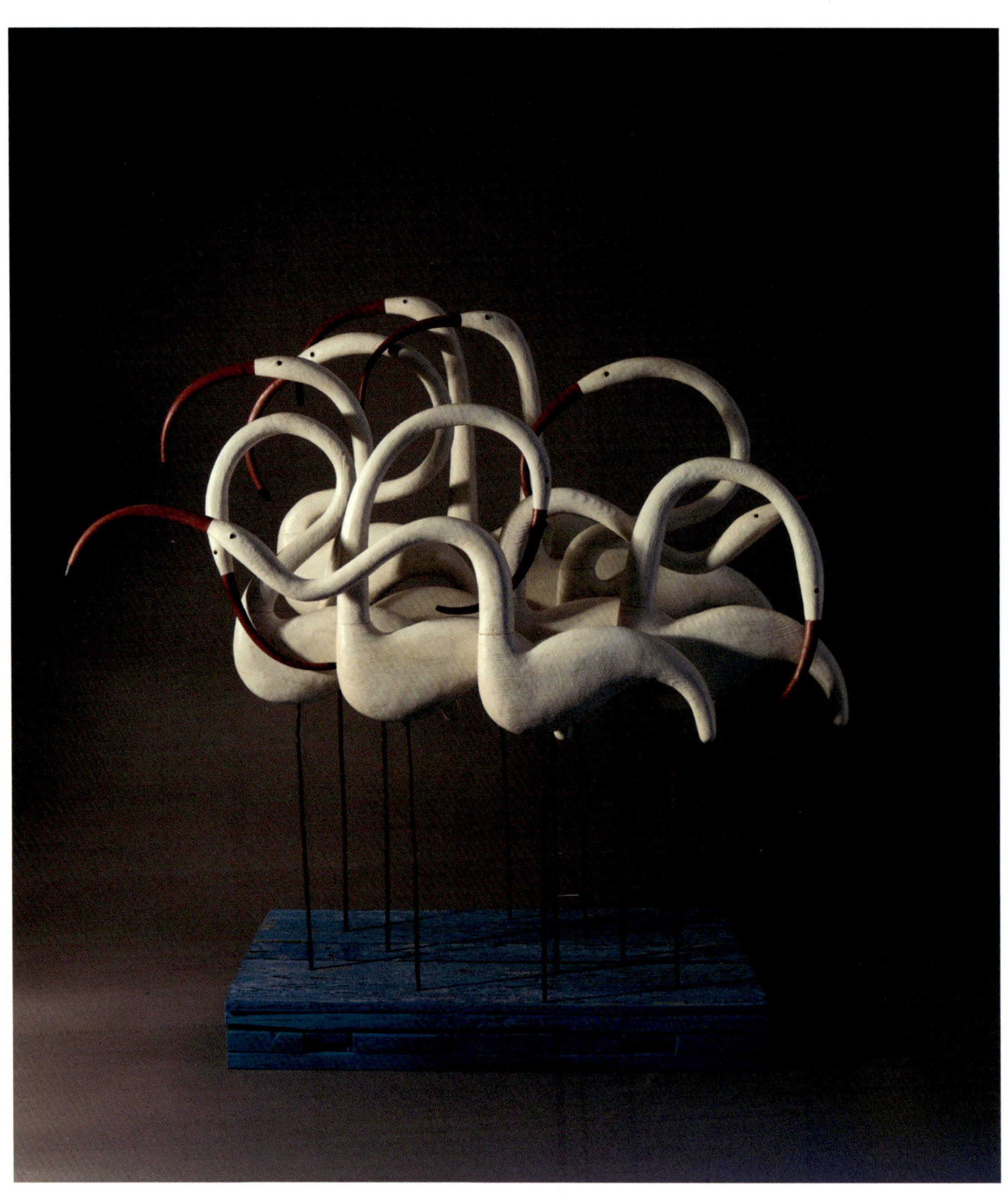

16. **TEN IBIS**
carved and painted driftwood
86 x 92 x 43 cms 33⅝ x 36¼ x 16⅞ ins

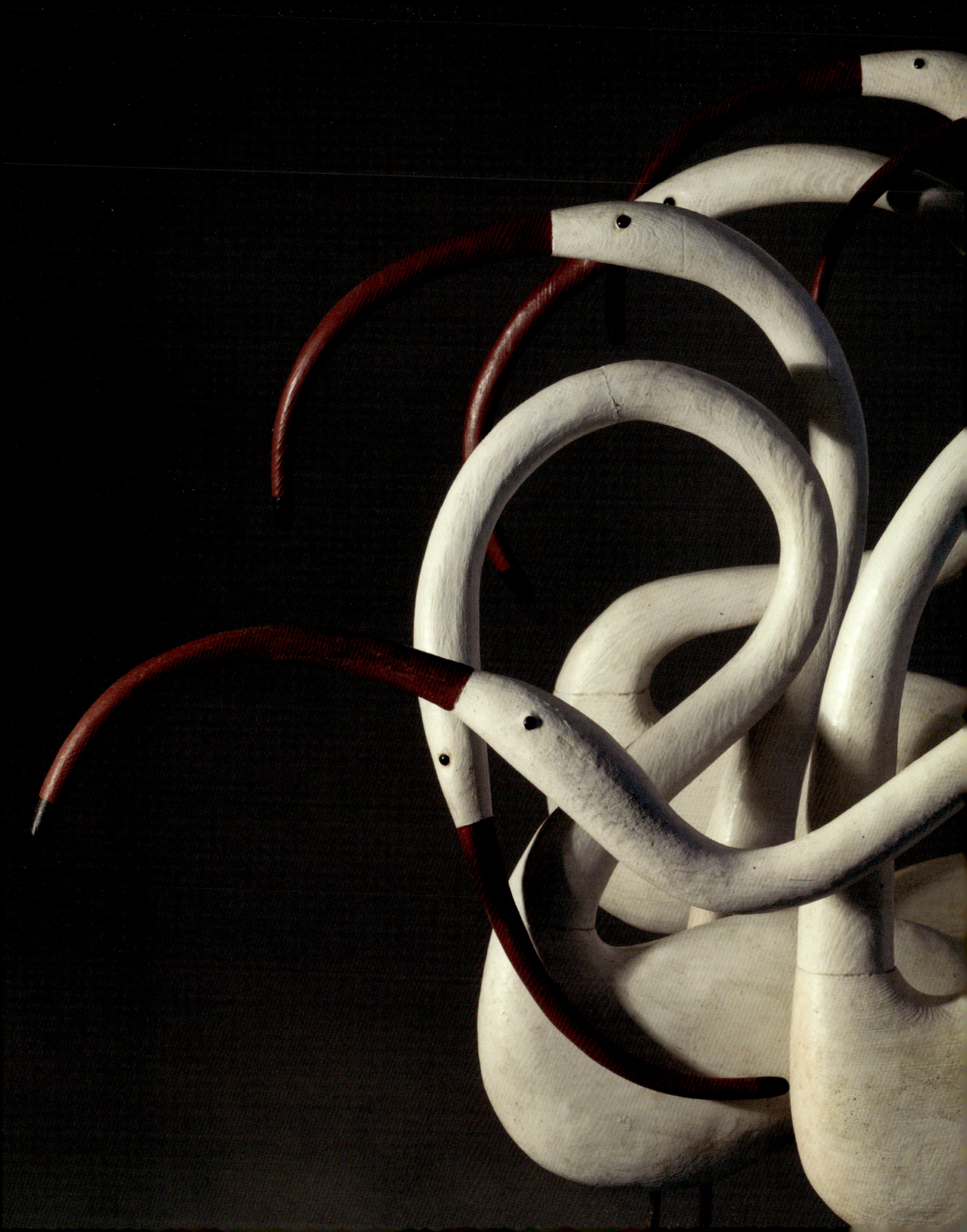

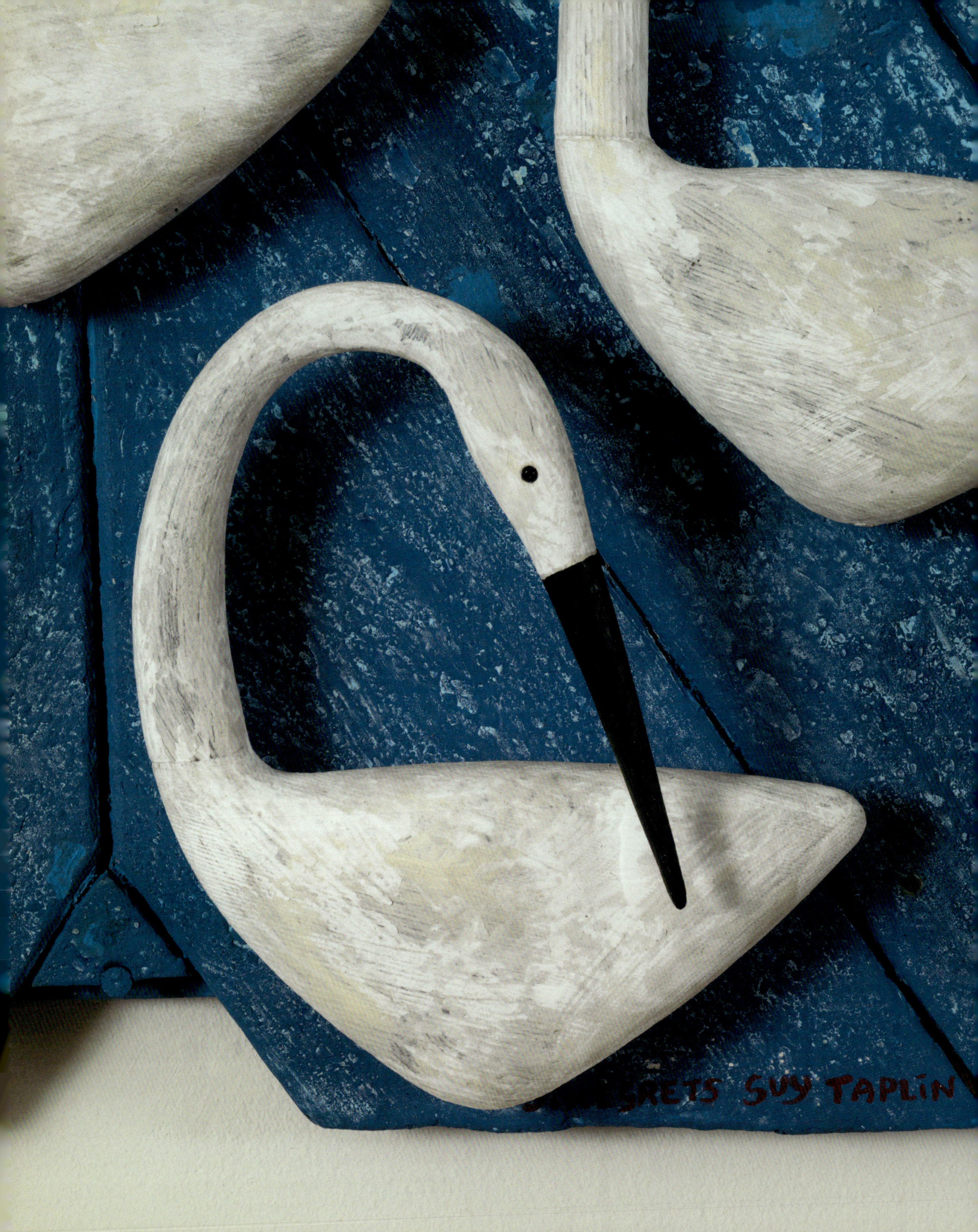
GUY TAPLIN

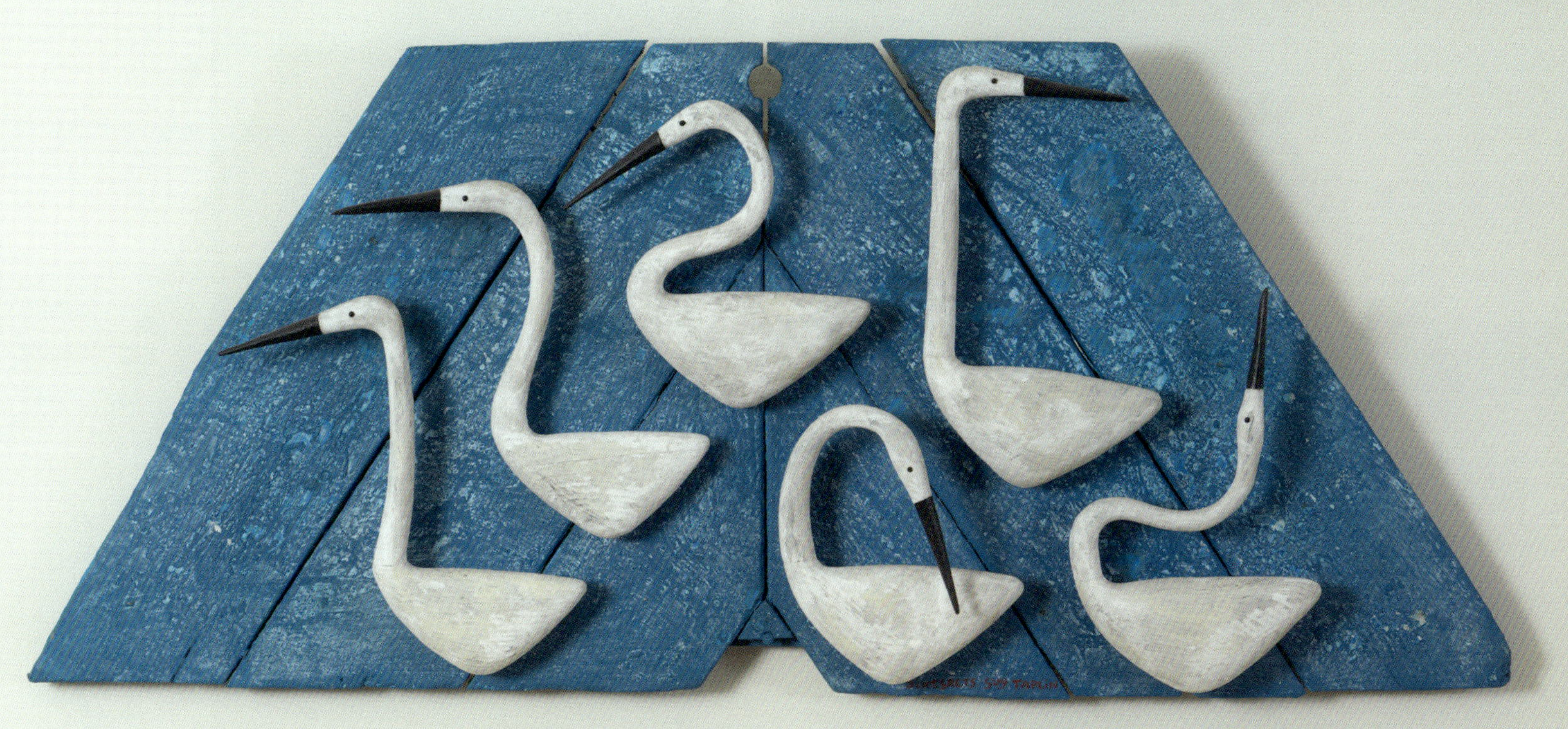

17. Six Egrets on a Panel
carved and painted driftwood
47 x 112 x 14 cms 18½ x 44⅛ x 5½ ins

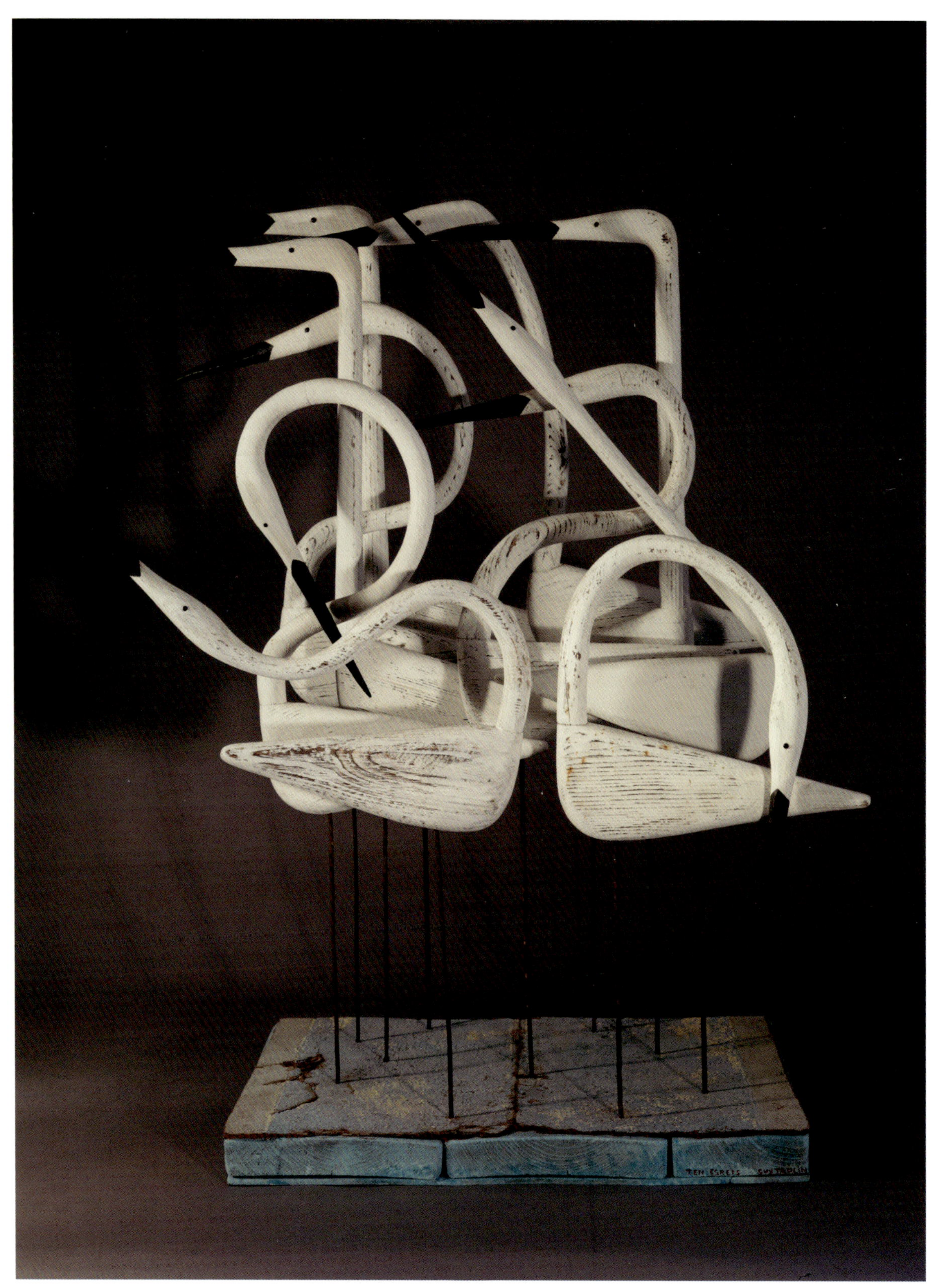

18. **Ten Egrets**
carved and painted driftwood
98 x 84 x 43 cms   38⅝ x 33⅛ x 16⅞ ins

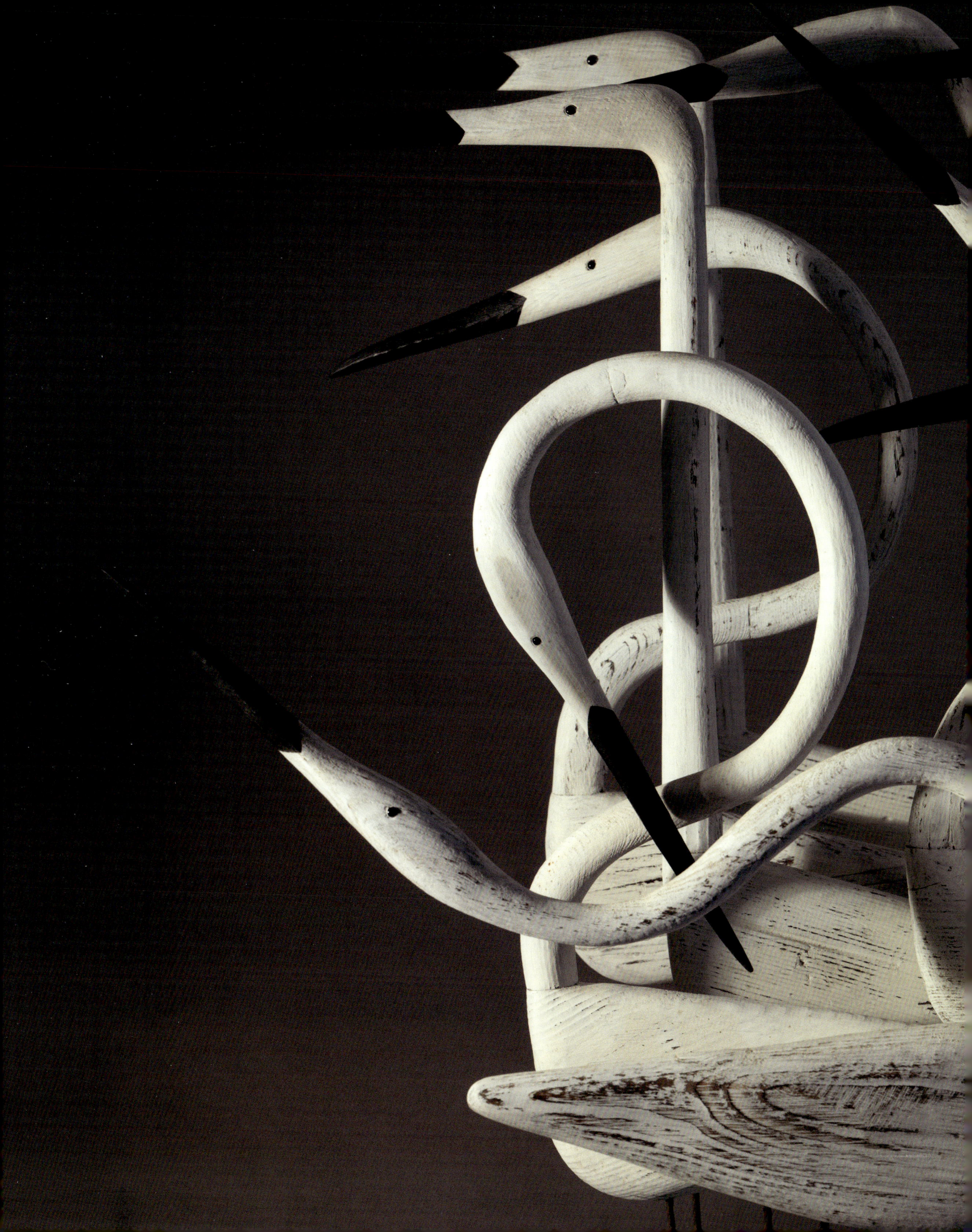

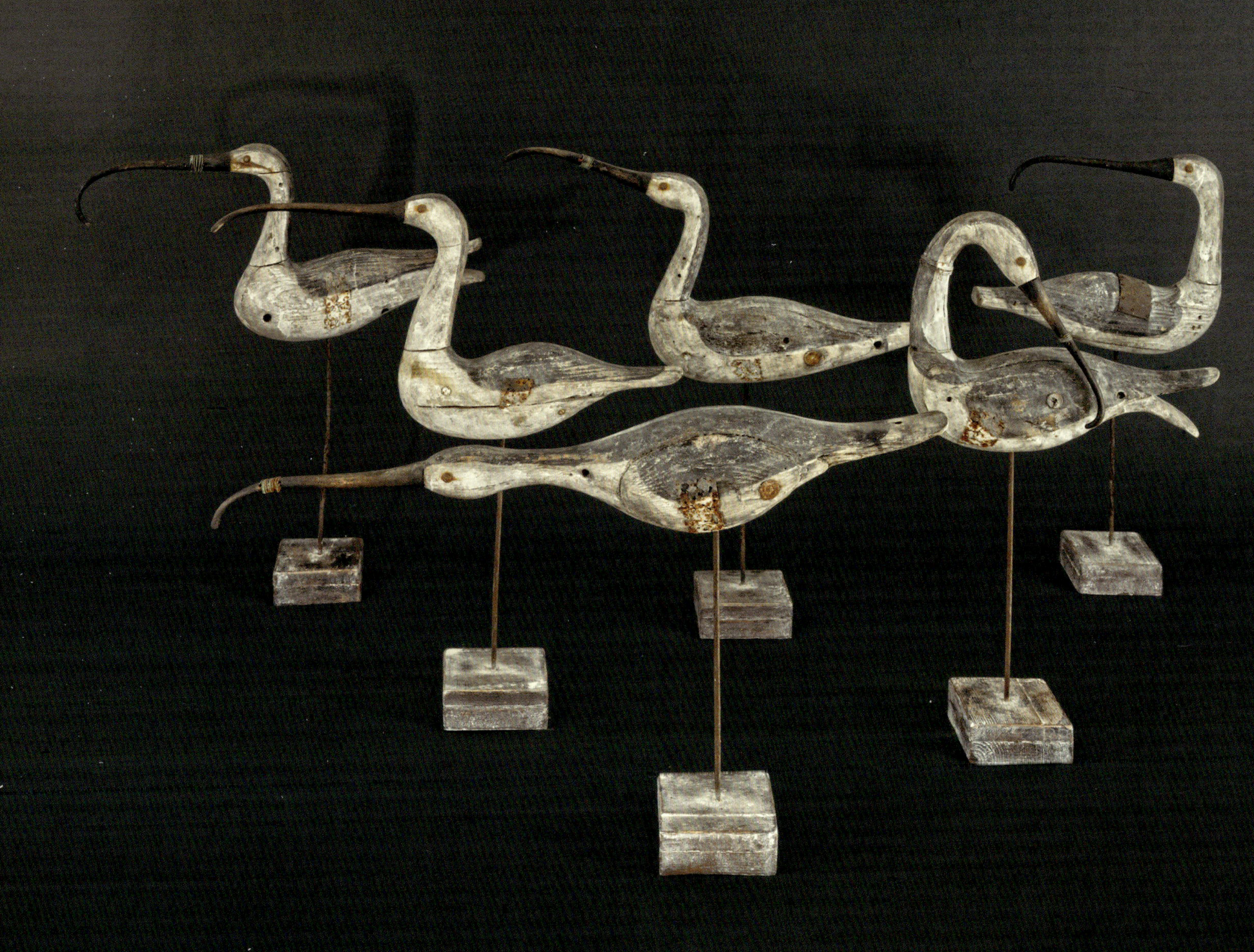

19. Group of Six Individual Curlews
carved and painted driftwood
average size: 66.5 x 62 x 12.5 cms   26 x 24 x 5 ins

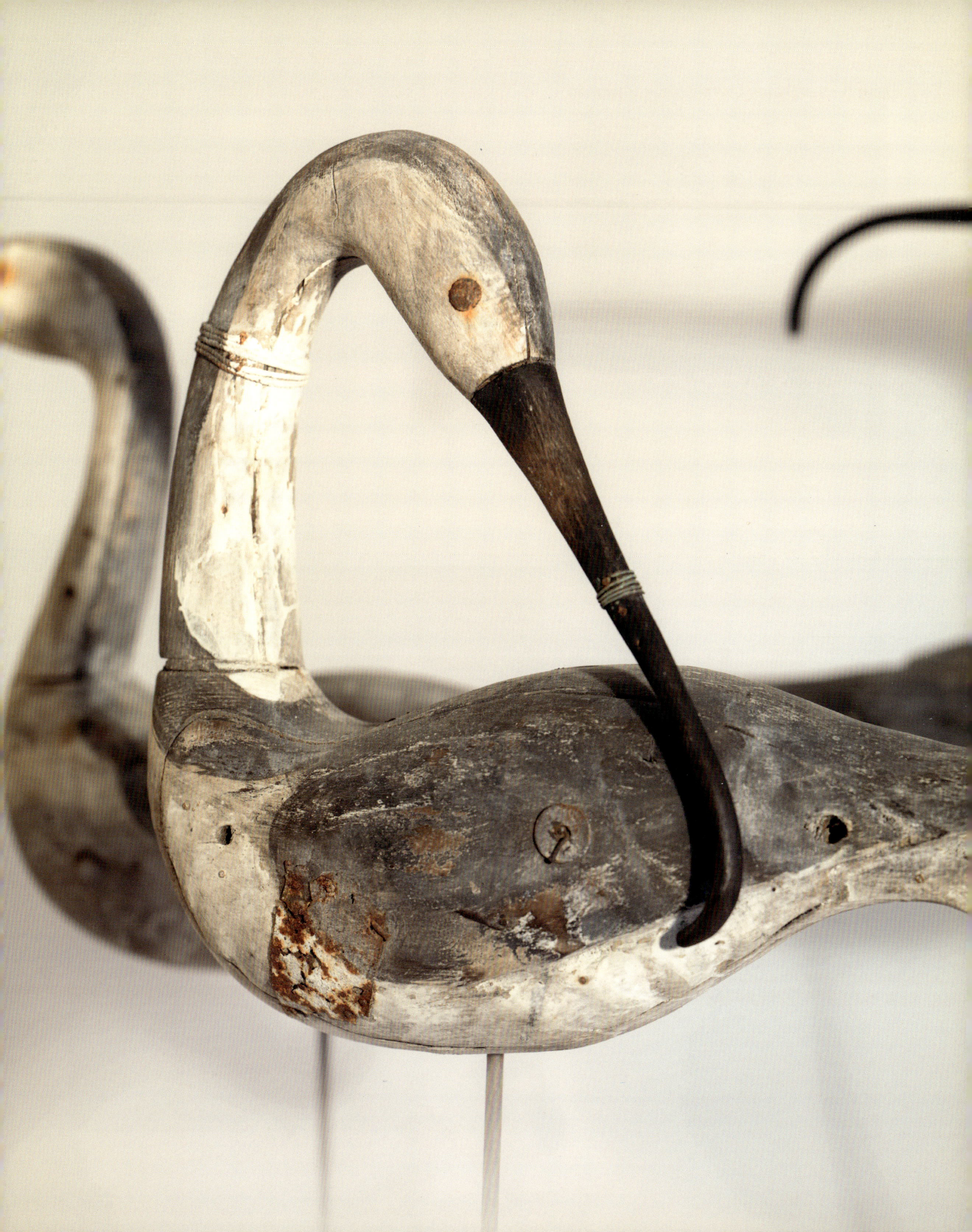

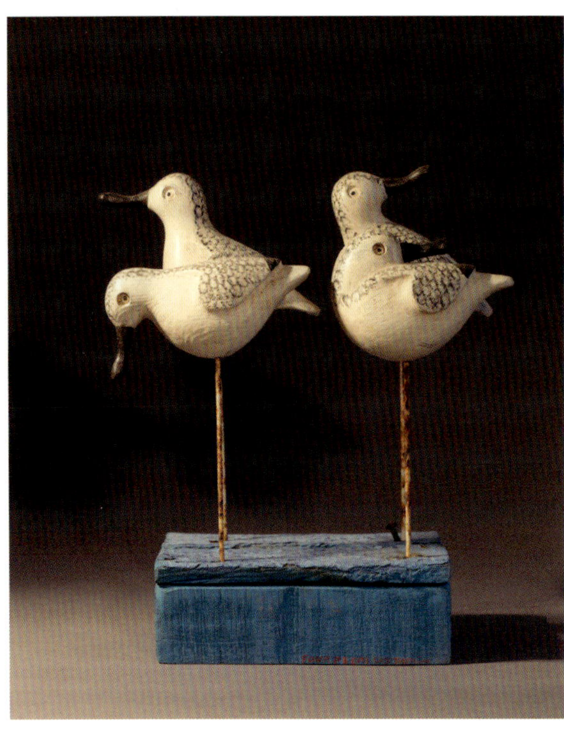

20. FOUR PEEPS
carved and painted driftwood
31 x 27 x 7 cms   12¼ x 10⅝ x 2½ ins

21. FOUR PLOVER
carved and painted driftwood
60 x 58 x 25 cms   23⅜ x 23 x 9⅞ ins

22. FOUR OYSTER CATCHERS (opposite)
carved and painted driftwood
91 x 70 x 57 cms   35⅞ x 27½ x 22½ ins

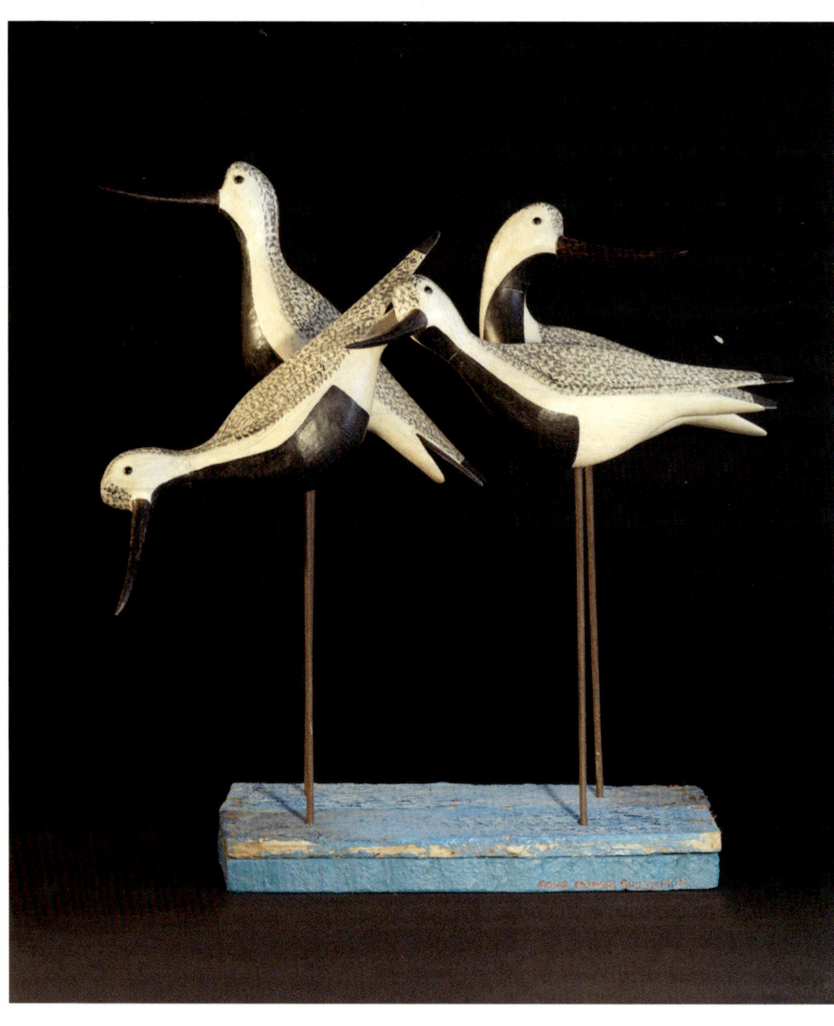

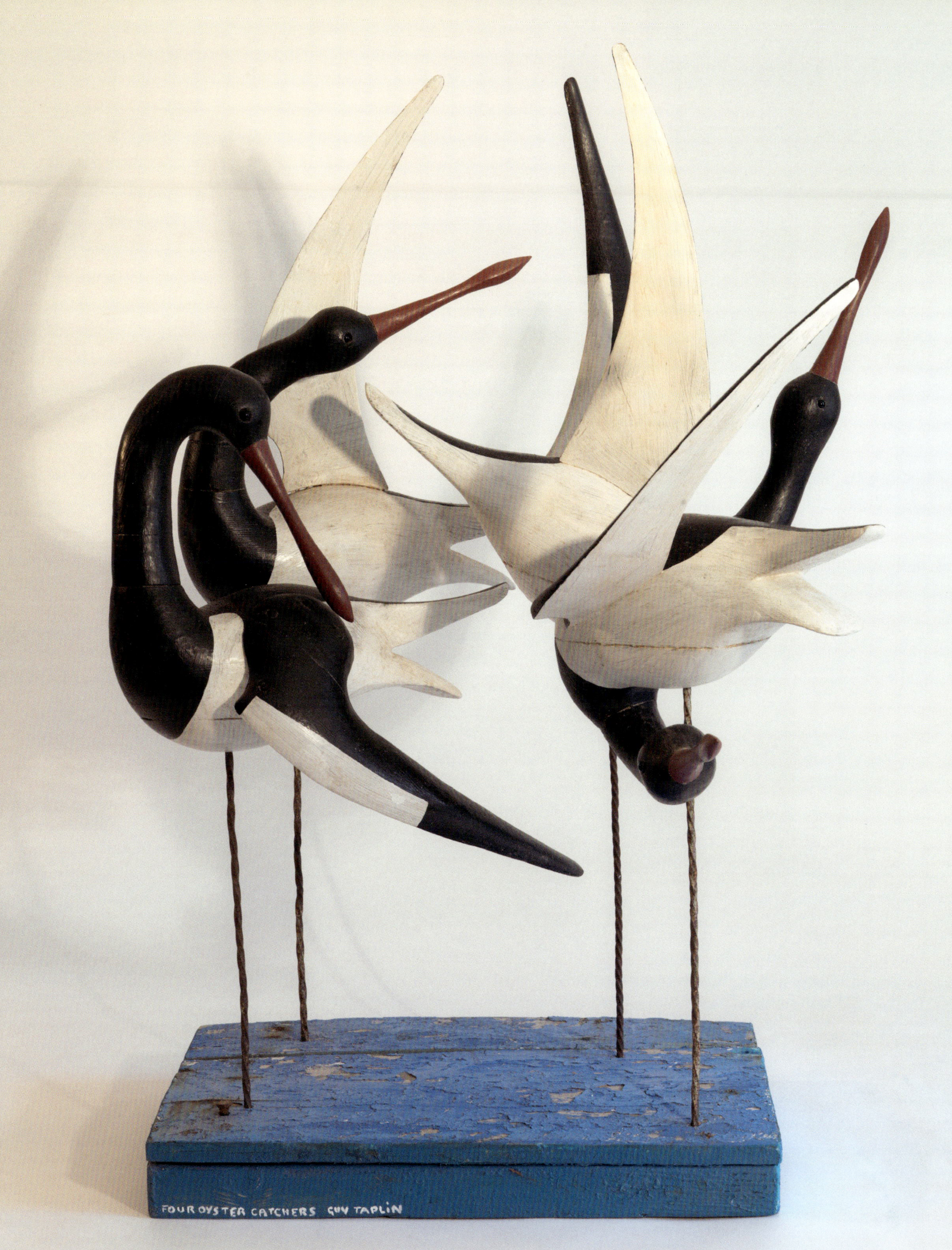
FOUR OYSTER CATCHERS GUY TAPLIN

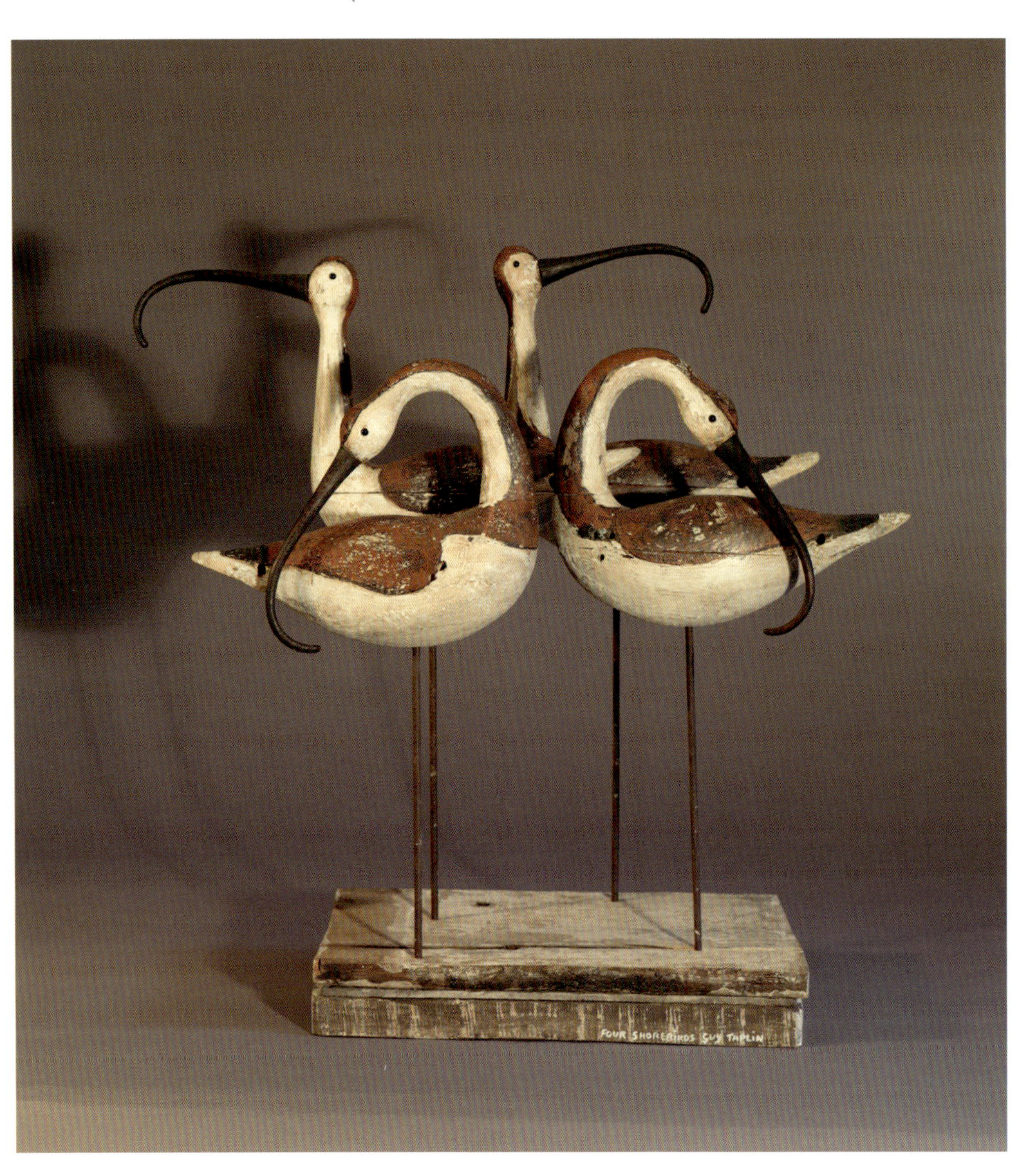

23. **Four Shorebirds**
carved and painted driftwood
62 x 64 x 33 cms   24⅜ x 25¼ x 13 ins

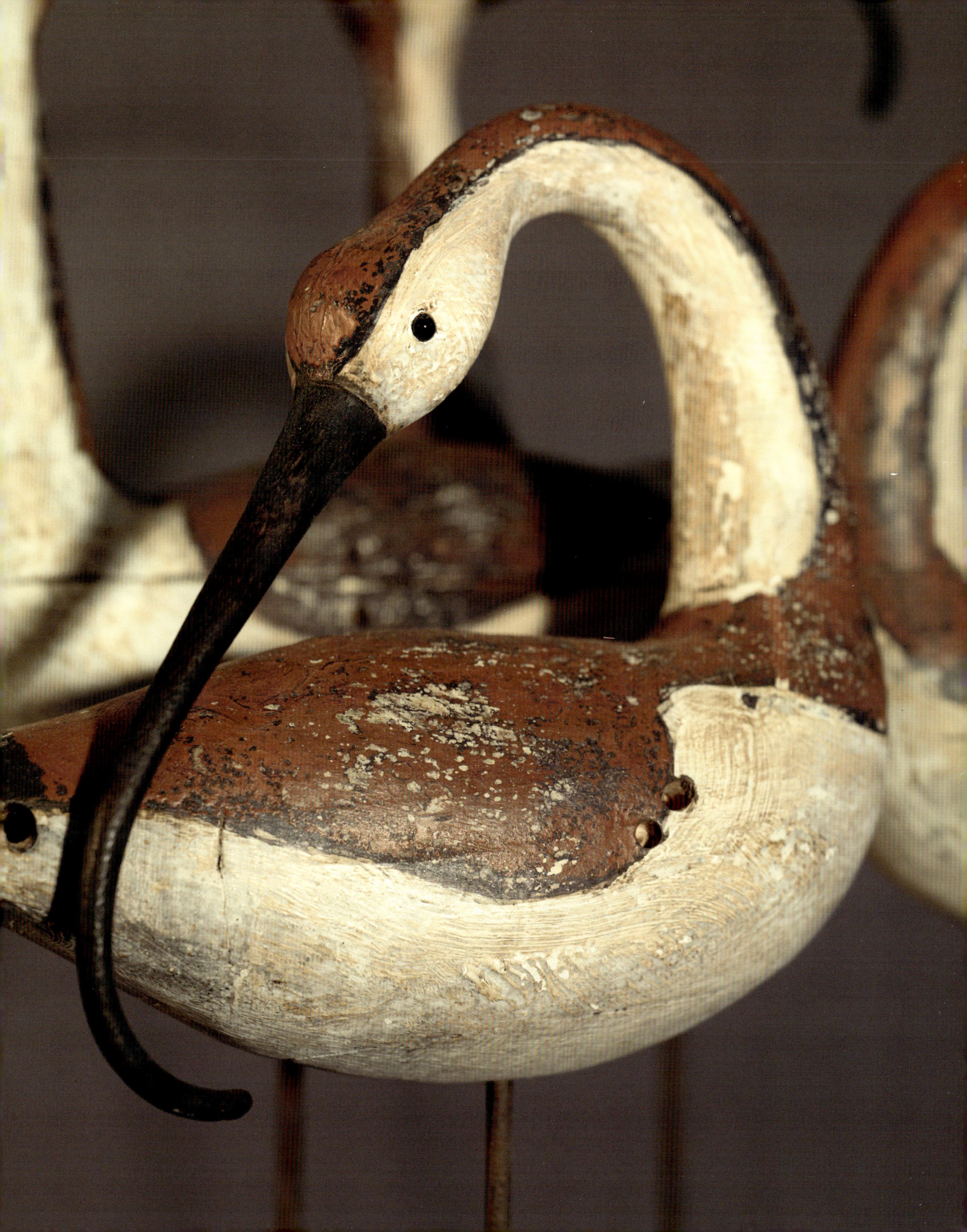

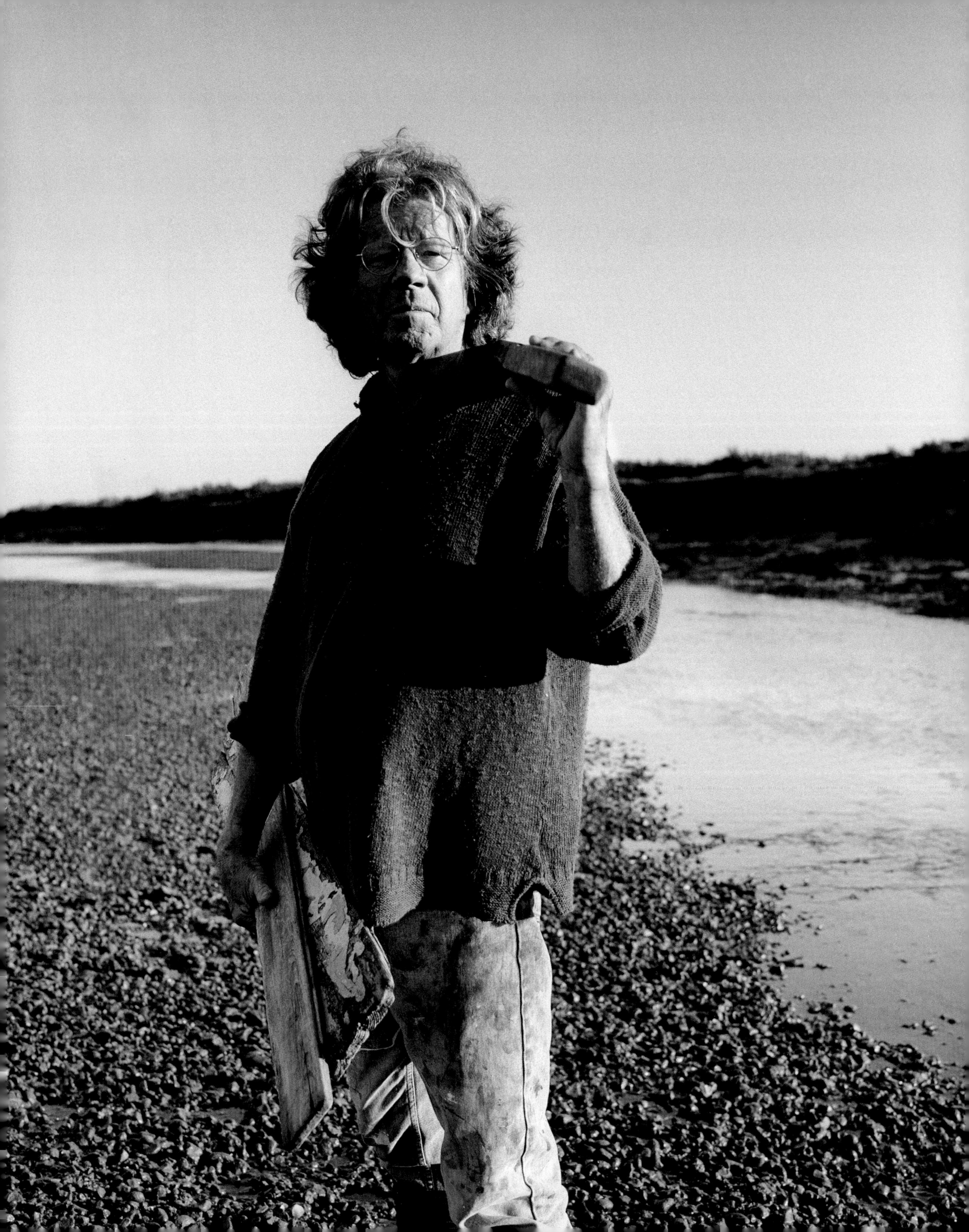

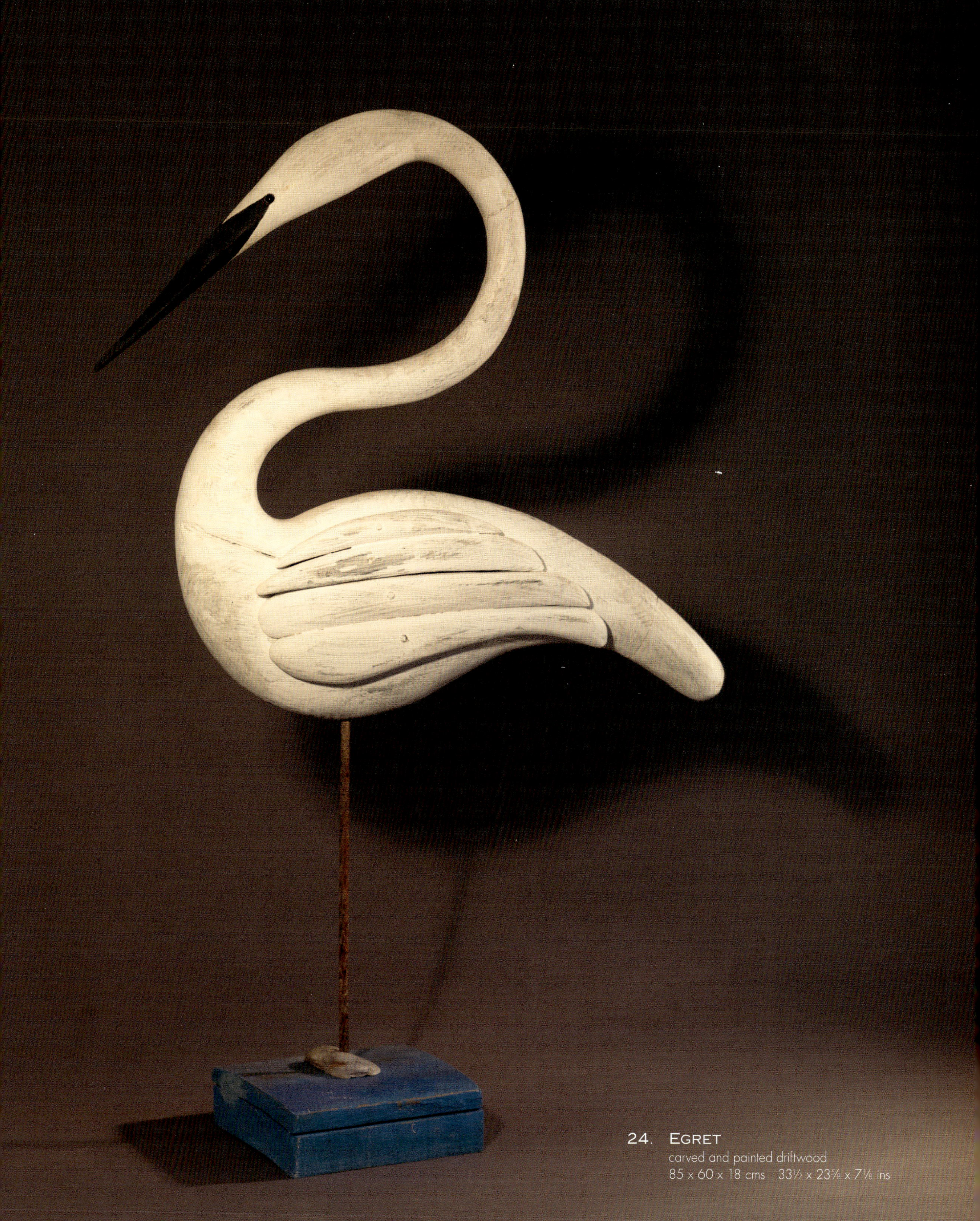

24. EGRET
carved and painted driftwood
85 x 60 x 18 cms   33½ x 23⅝ x 7⅛ ins

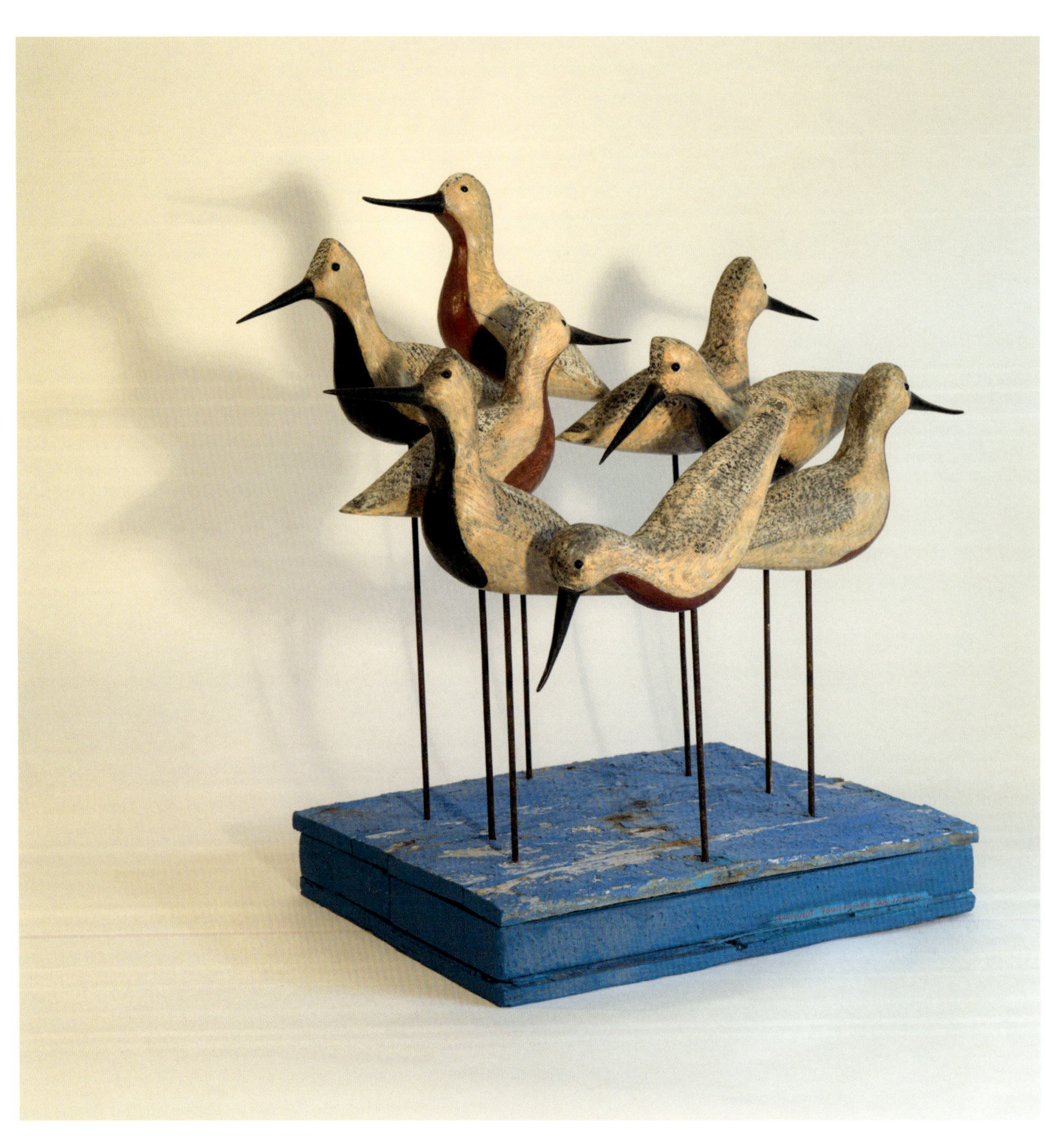

25. Four Knot, Four Plover
carved and painted driftwood
70 x 73 x 44 cms 27½ x 28¾ x 17⅜ ins

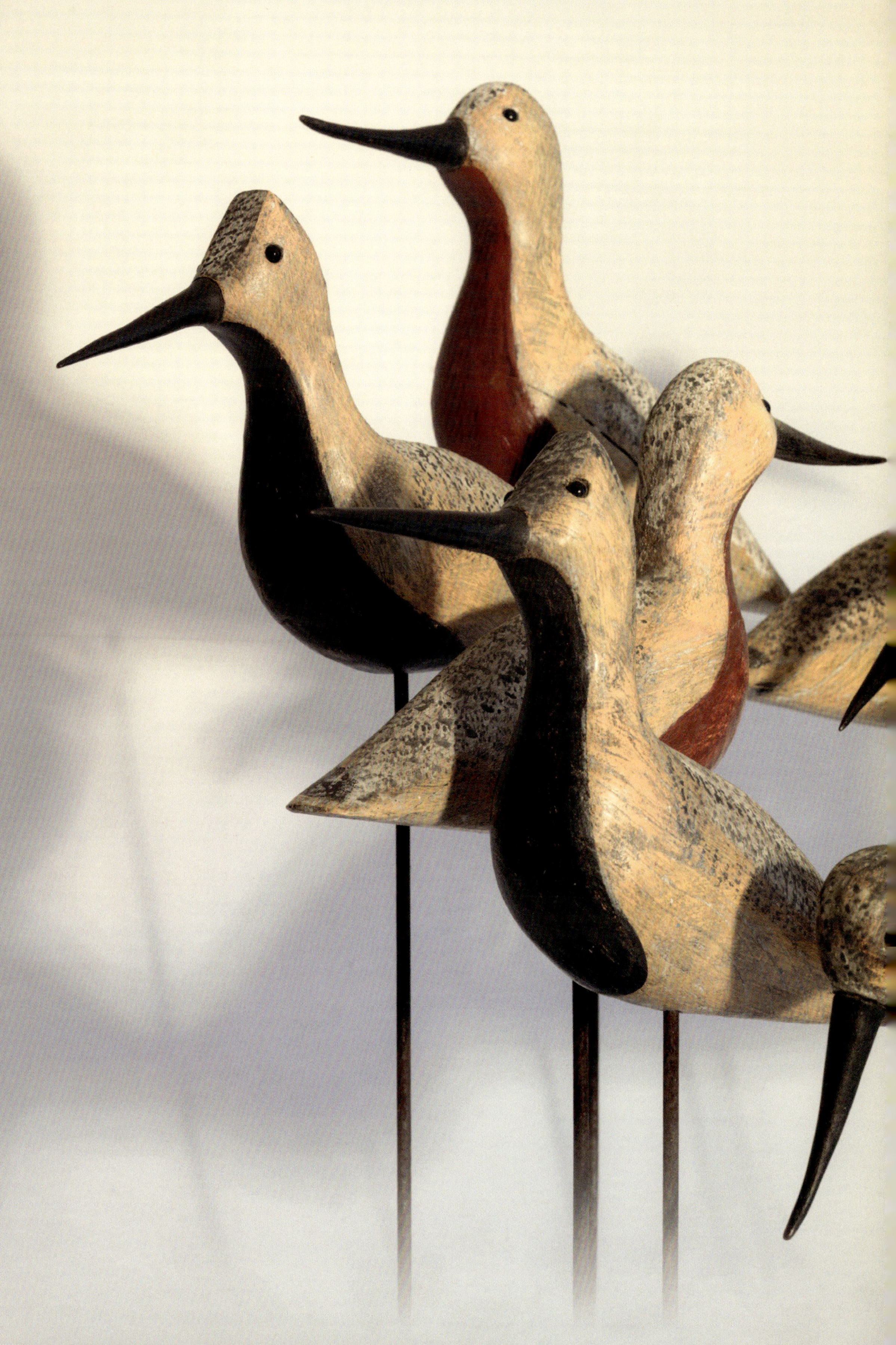

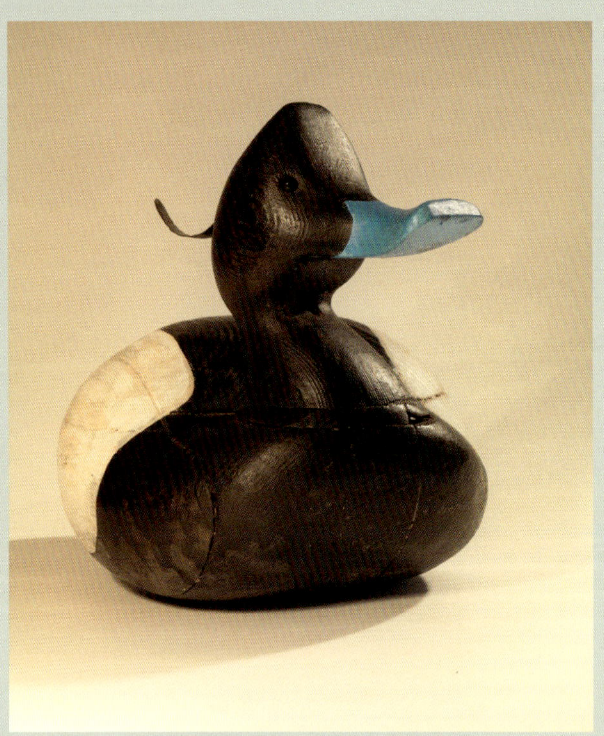

26. **Tufted Duck**
carved and painted driftwood
26 x 32 x 23 cms 10 x 12⅝ x 9 ins

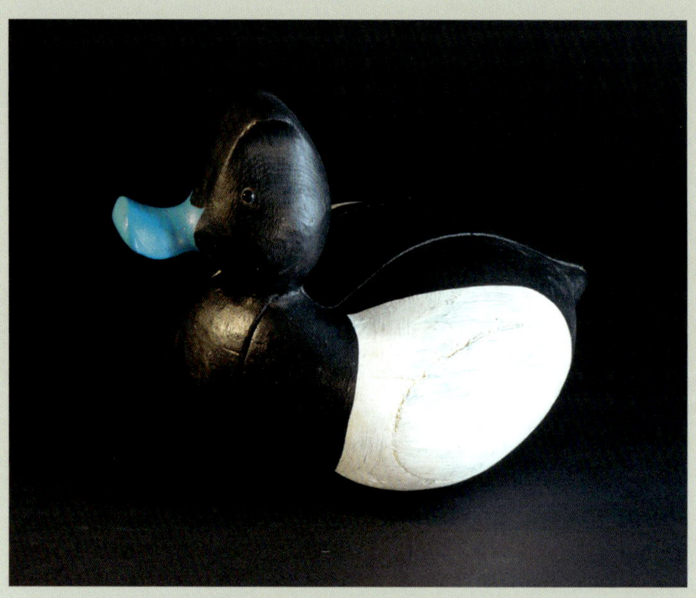

27. **Scaup**
carved and painted driftwood
26 x 36 x 25 cms 10¼ x 14⅛ x 9⅝ ins

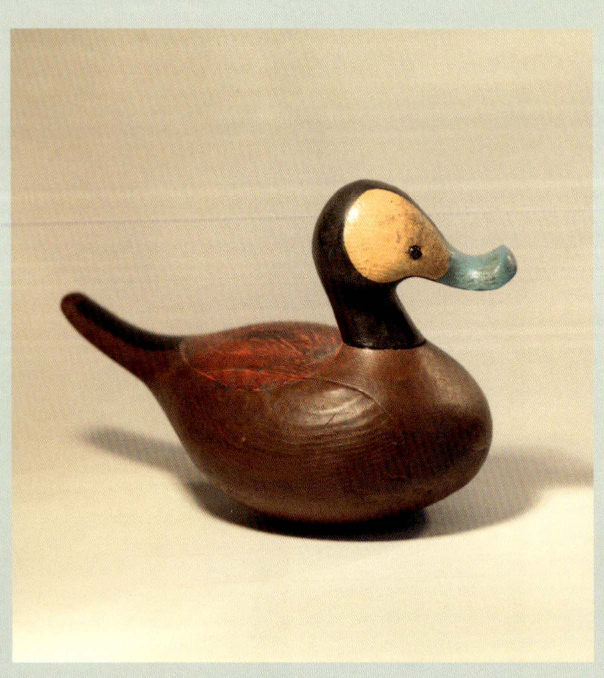

28. **Ruddy Duck**
carved and painted driftwood
22 x 33 x 18 cms 8½ x 13 x 6⅞ ins

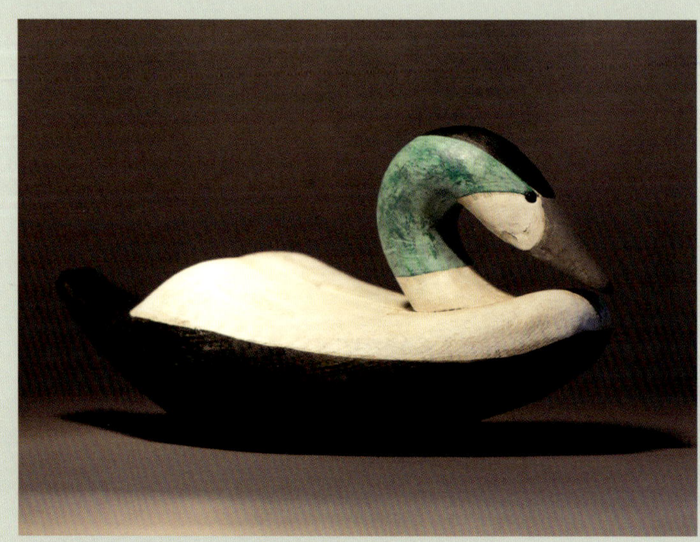

29. **Eider** (detail opposite)
carved and painted driftwood
23 x 51 x 25 cms 9 x 20⅛ x 9⅞ ins

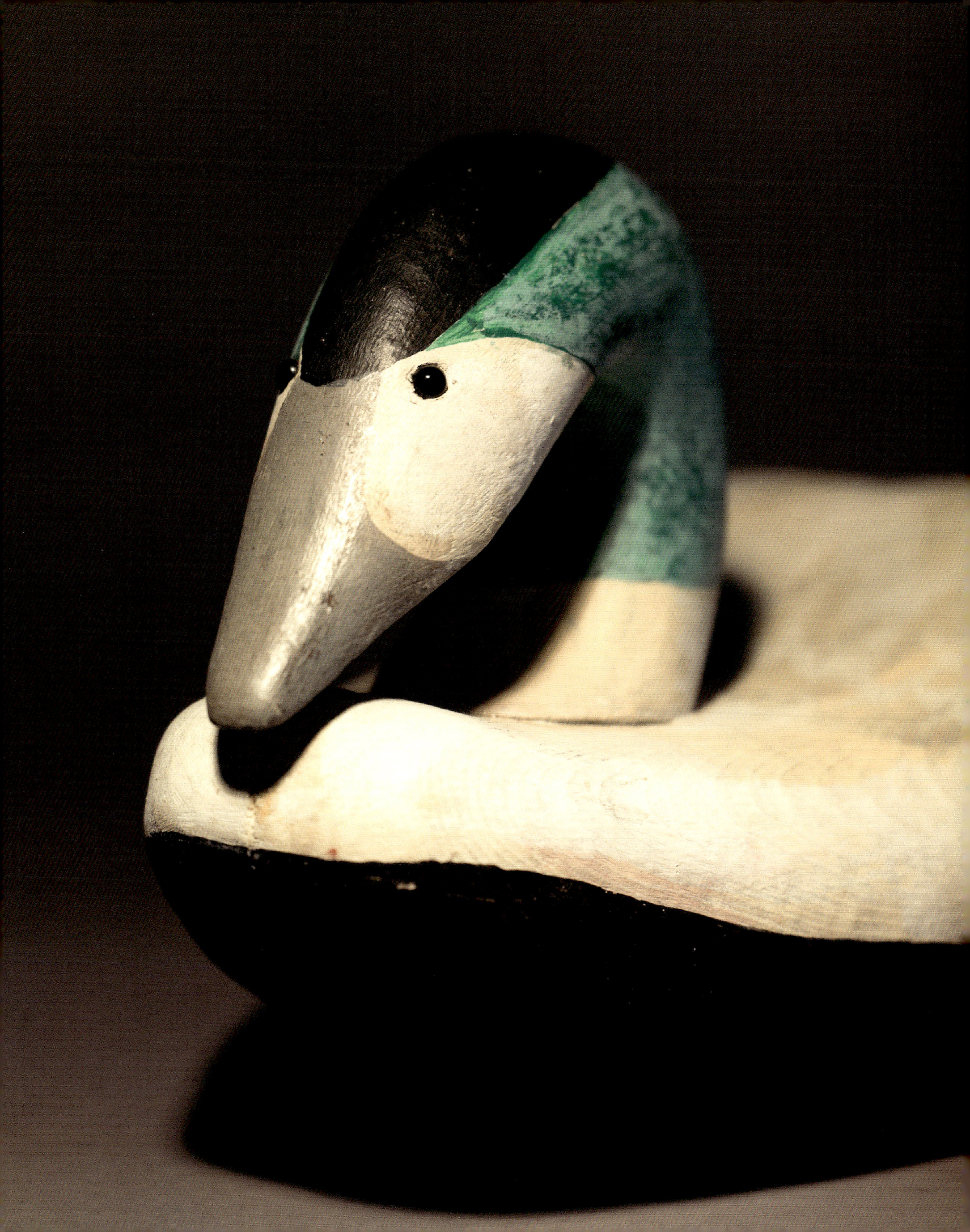

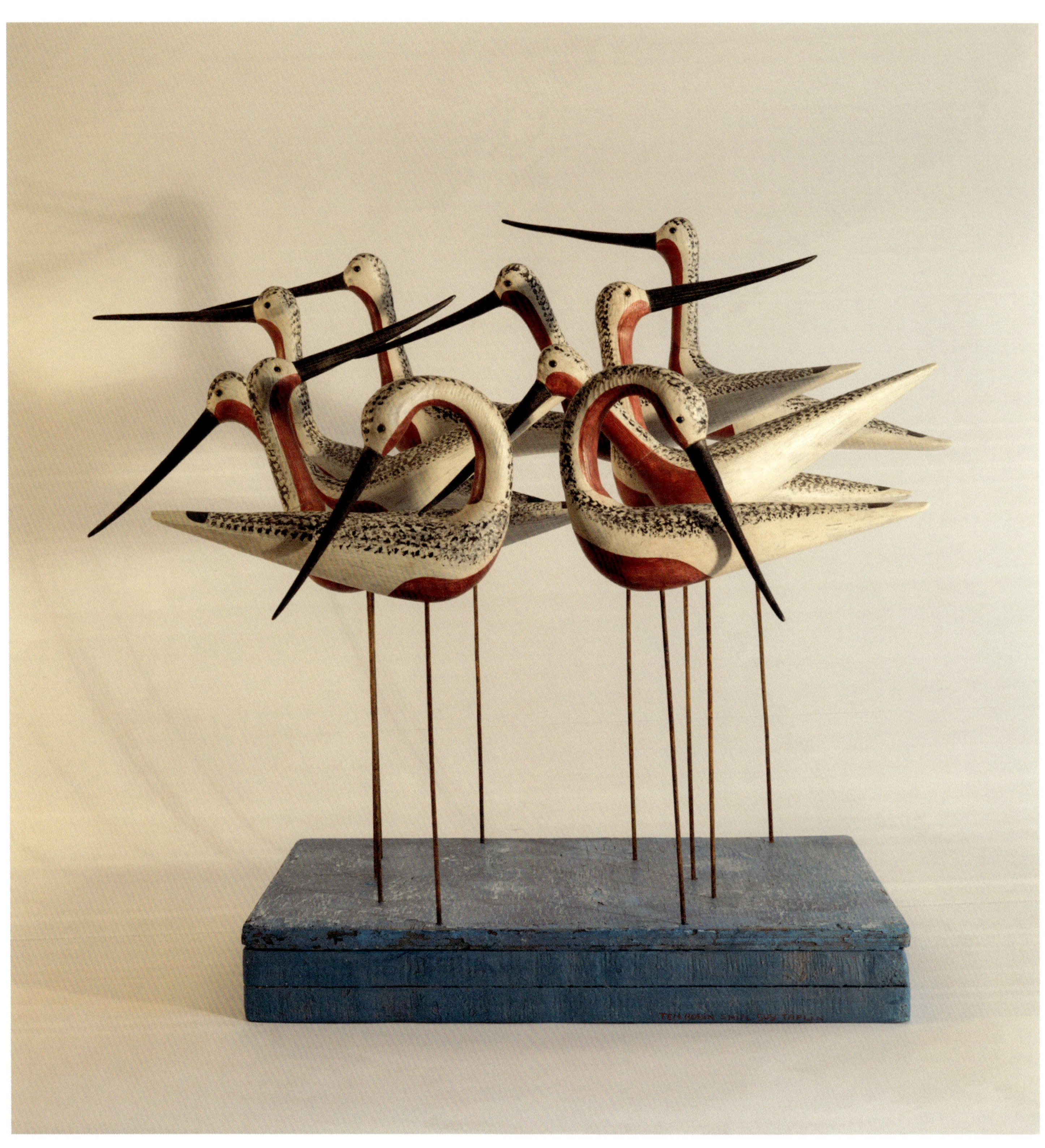

30. **Ten Knot**
carved and painted driftwood
67 x 80 x 45 cms   26⅛ x 31½ x 17¾ ins

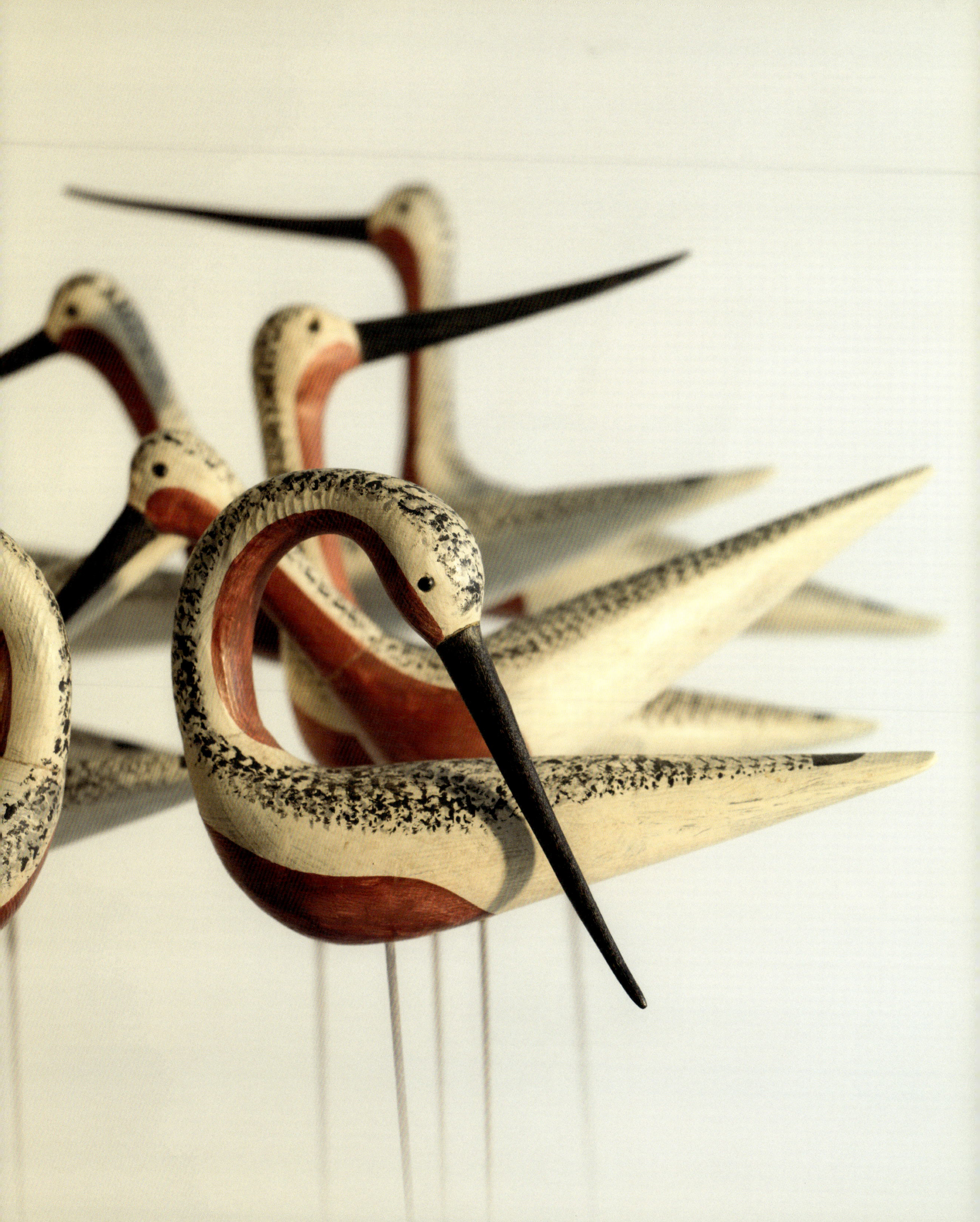

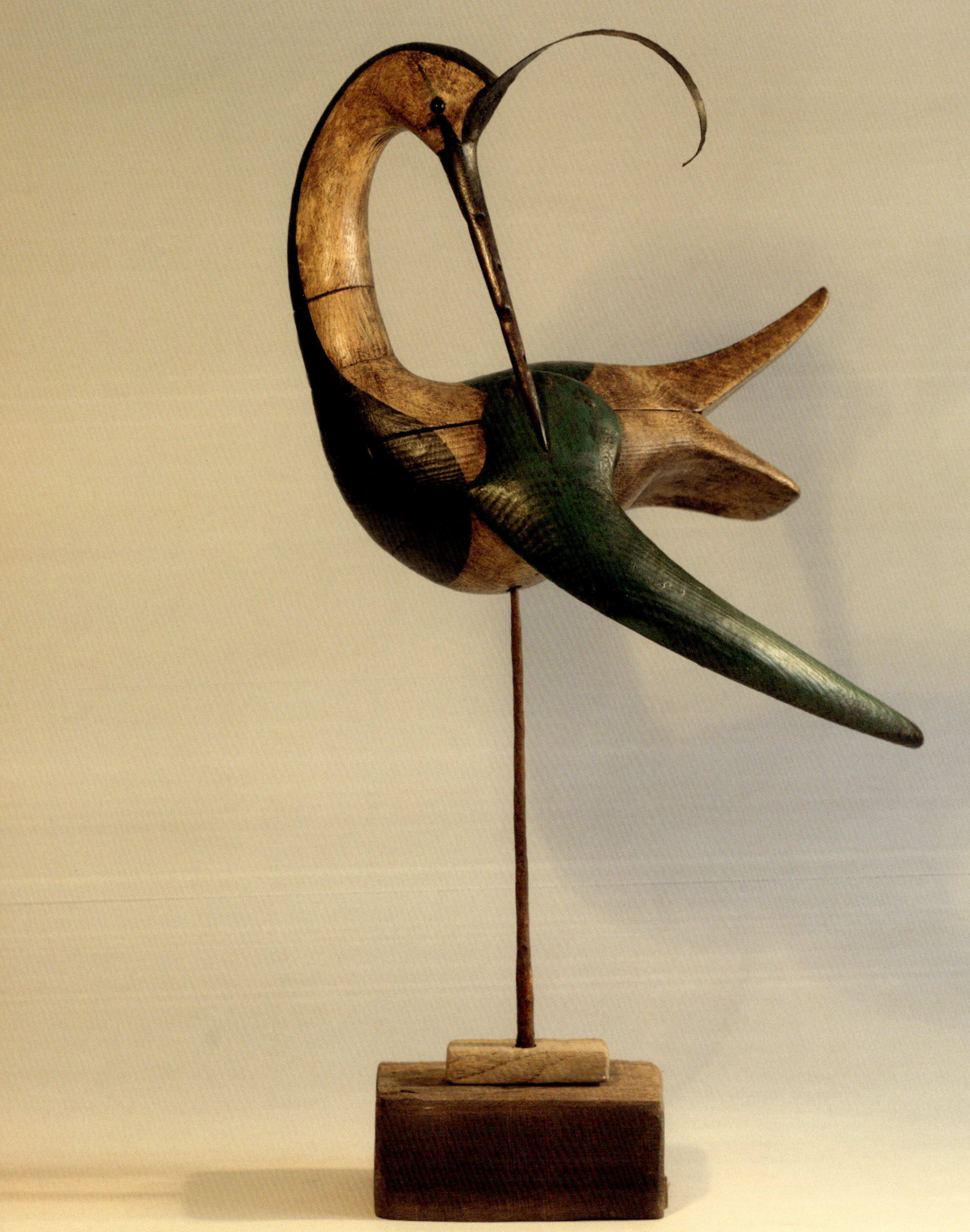

31. Lapwing
carved and painted driftwood
63 x 35 x 24 cms 24¾ x 13¾ x 9½ ins

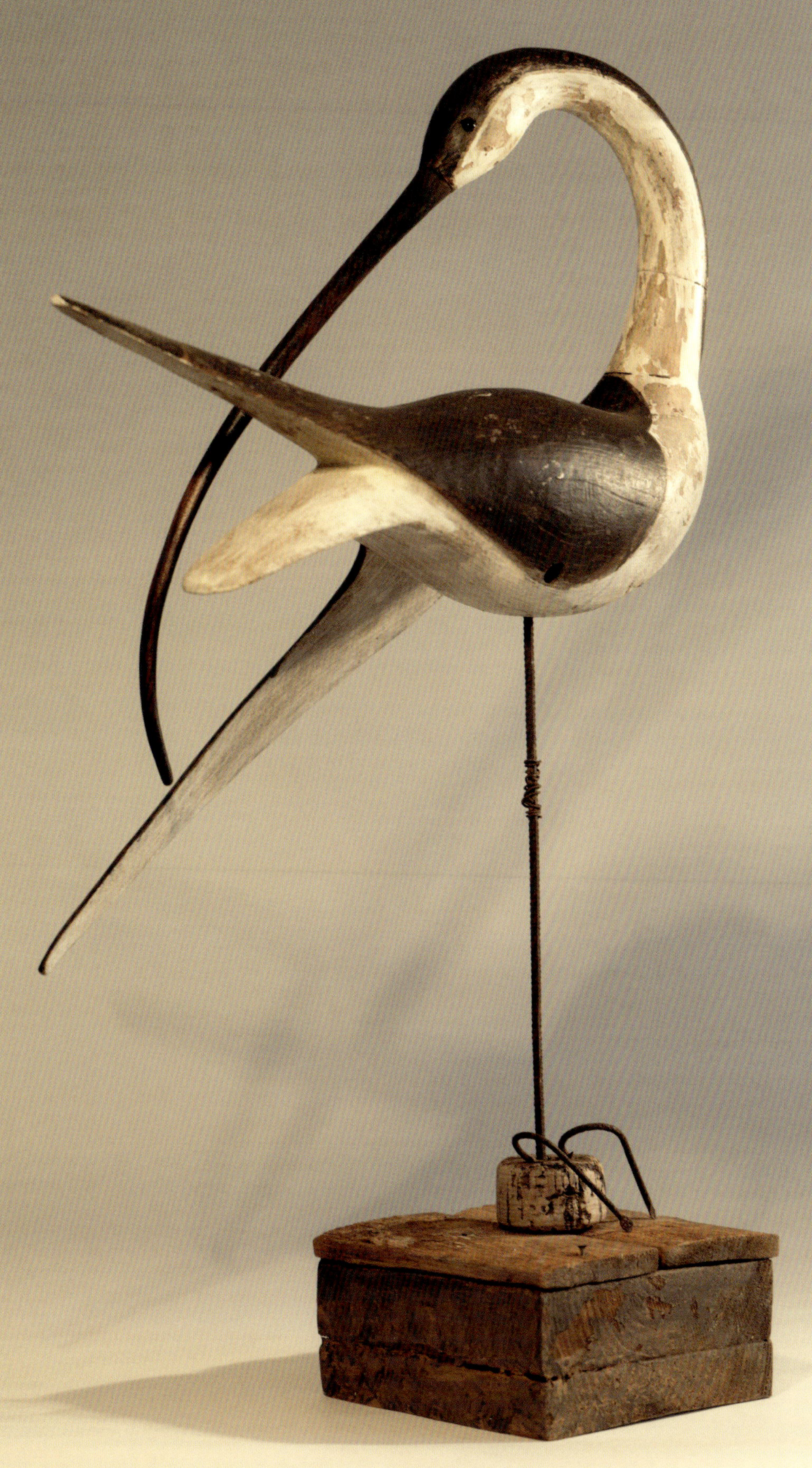

32. CURLEW
carved and painted driftwood
80 x 46 x 29 cms   31½ x 18⅛ x 11⅜ ins

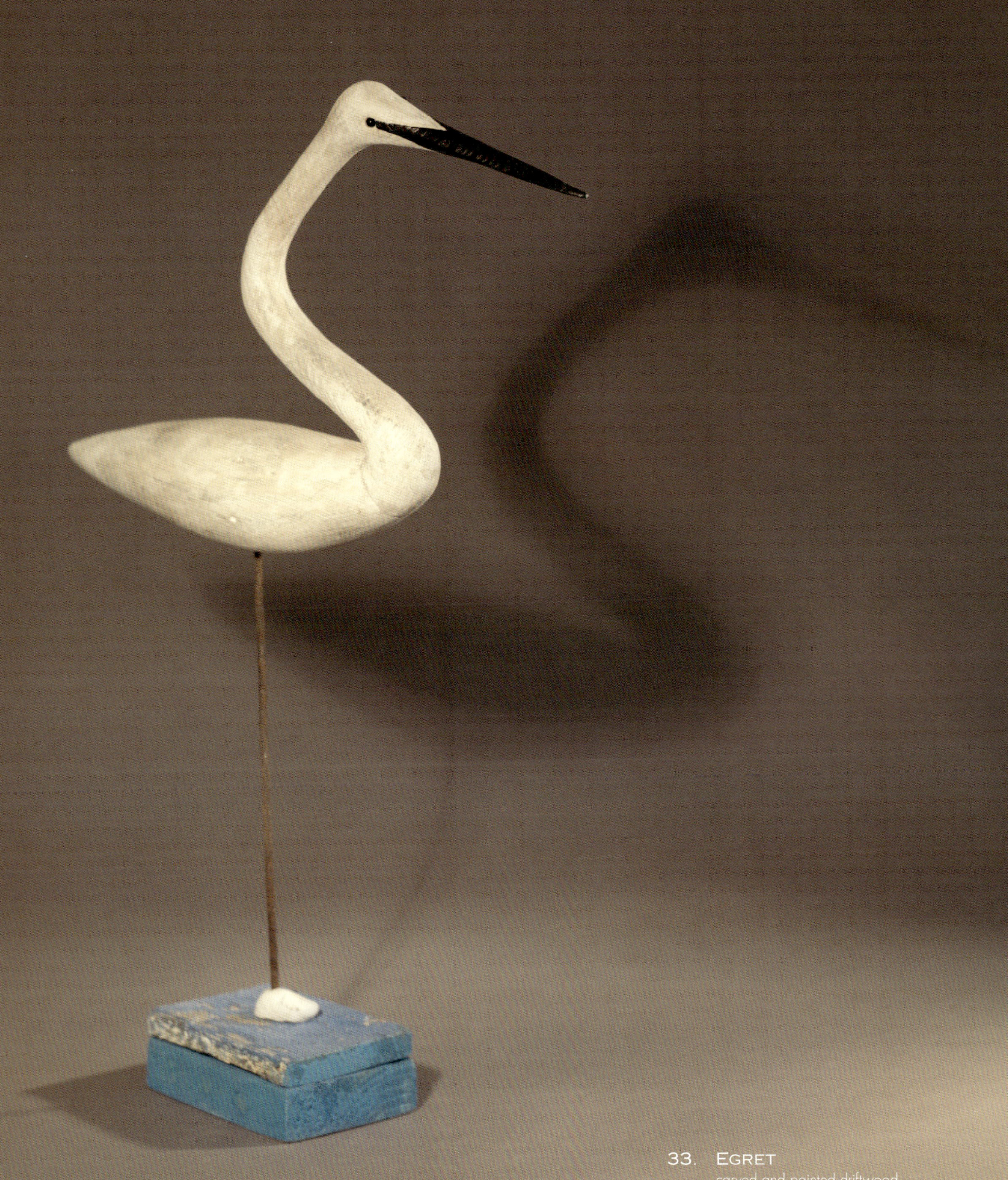

33. Egret
carved and painted driftwood
65 x 43 x 11 cms   25⅝ x 16⅞ x 4⅛ ins

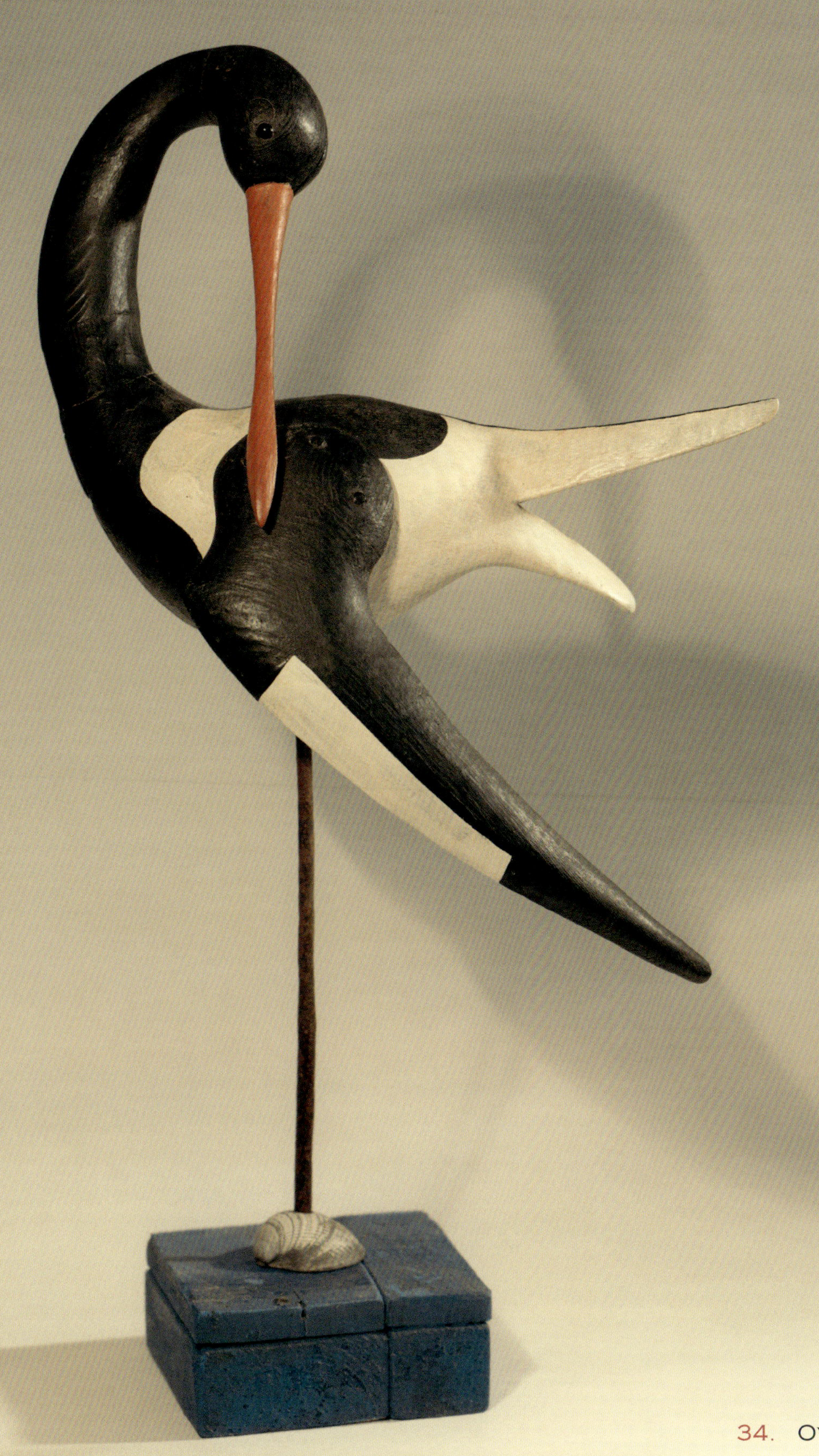

34. Oyster Catcher
carved and painted driftwood
65 x 36 x 20 cms 25⅝ x 14⅛ x 7⅞ ins

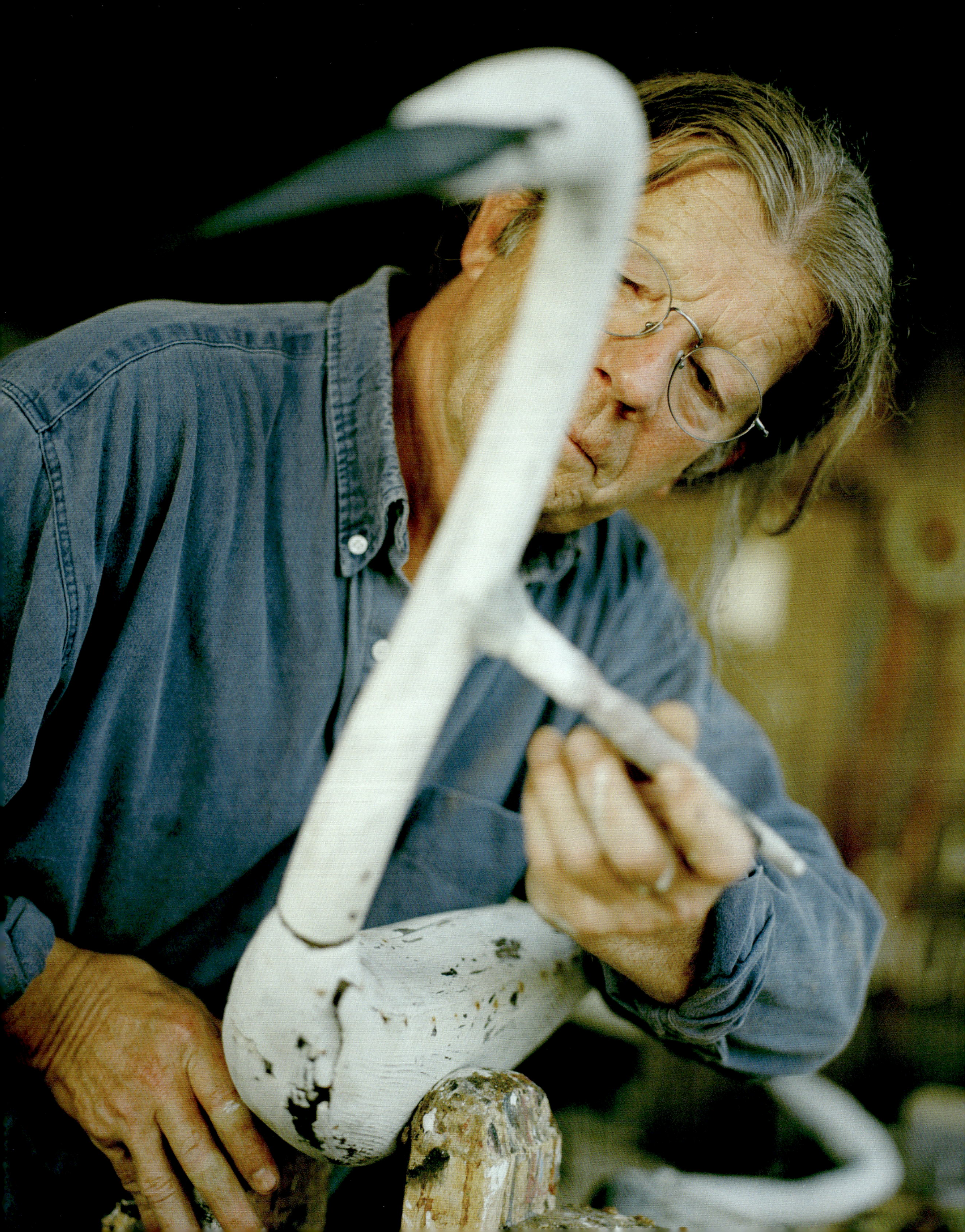

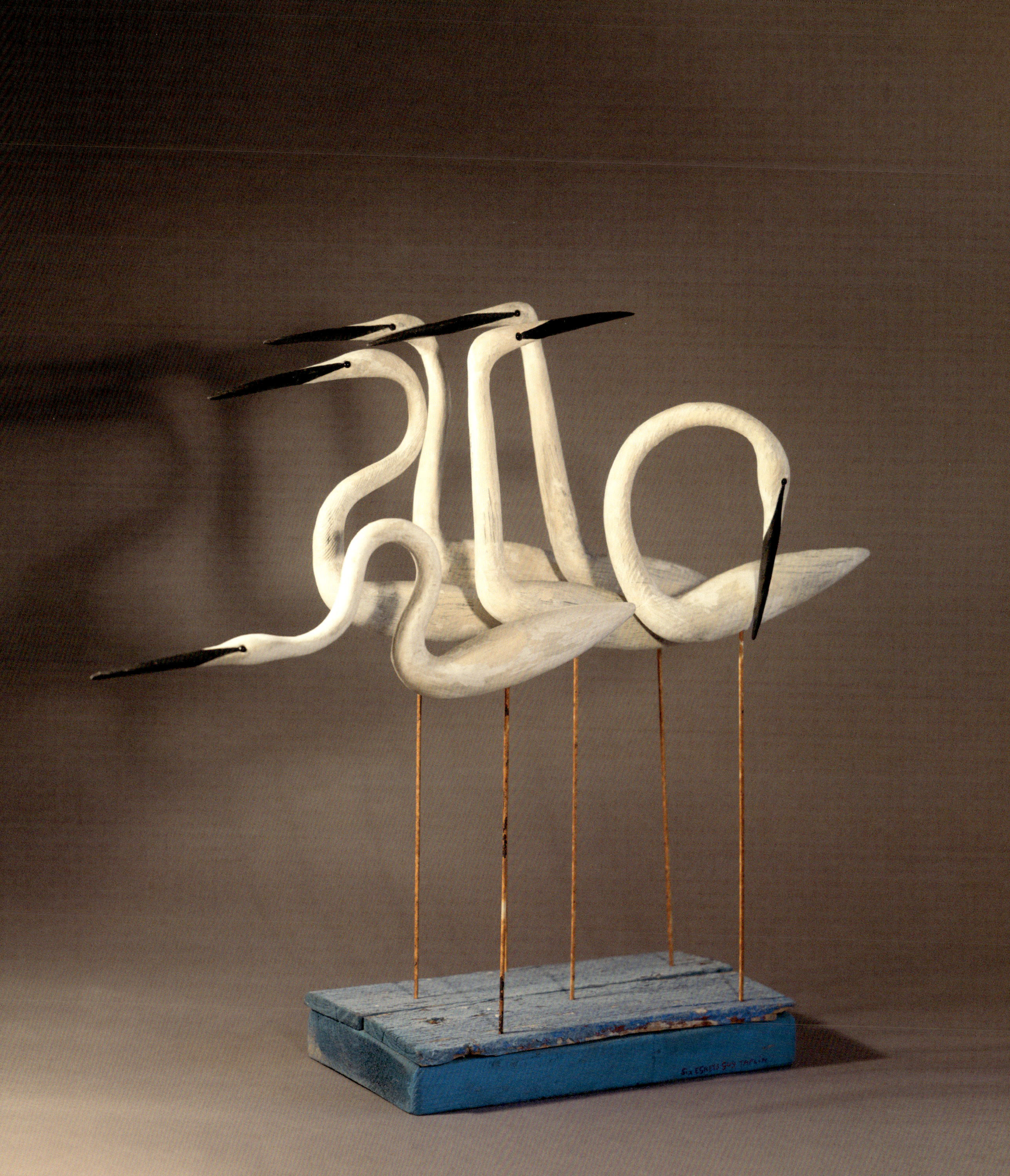

35. Six Egret
carved and painted driftwood
63 x 70 x 25 cms 24¾ x 27½ x 9⅞ ins

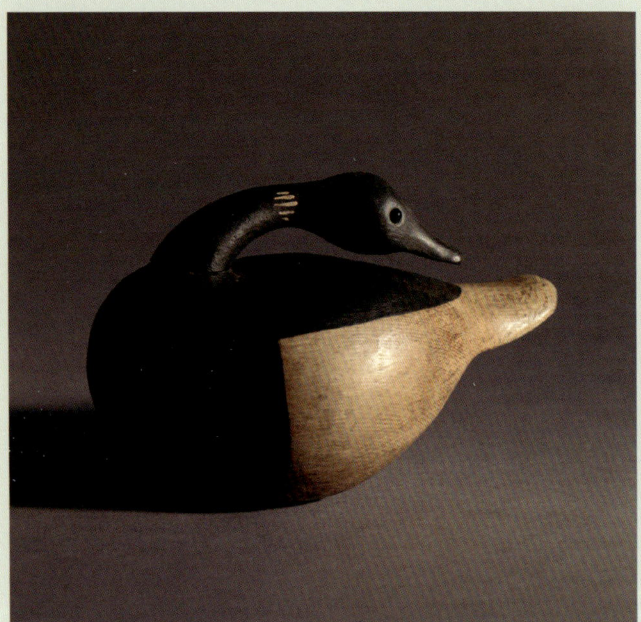

36. **Black Brent**
carved and painted driftwood
15 x 22 x 14 cms 5¾ x 8⅝ x 5½ ins

37. **Small Preening Mallard**
carved and painted driftwood
20 x 32 x 15 cms 7⅞ x 12⅝ x 5⅞ ins

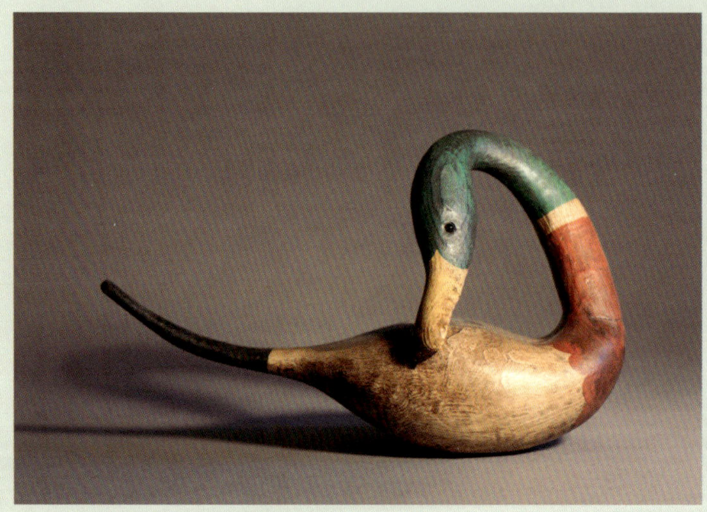

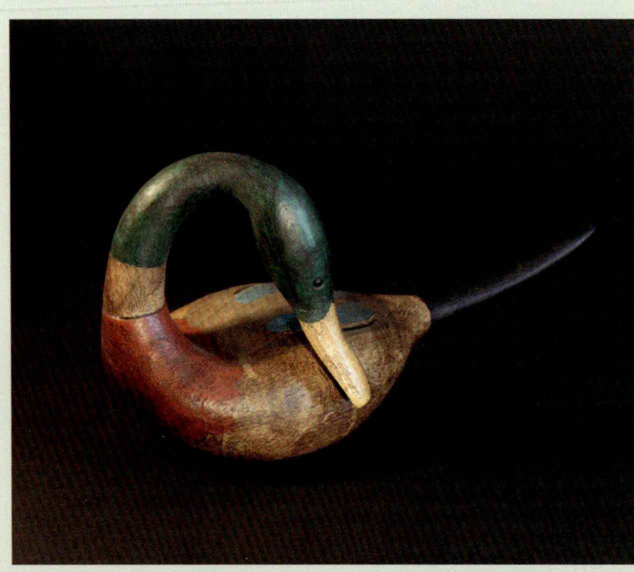

38. **Small Preening Mallard**
carved and painted driftwood
20 x 37 x 17 cms 7⅞ x 14⅝ x 6½ ins

39. **FOUR PLOVER**
carved and painted driftwood
47 x 45 x 23 cms 18½ x 17¾ x 9 ins

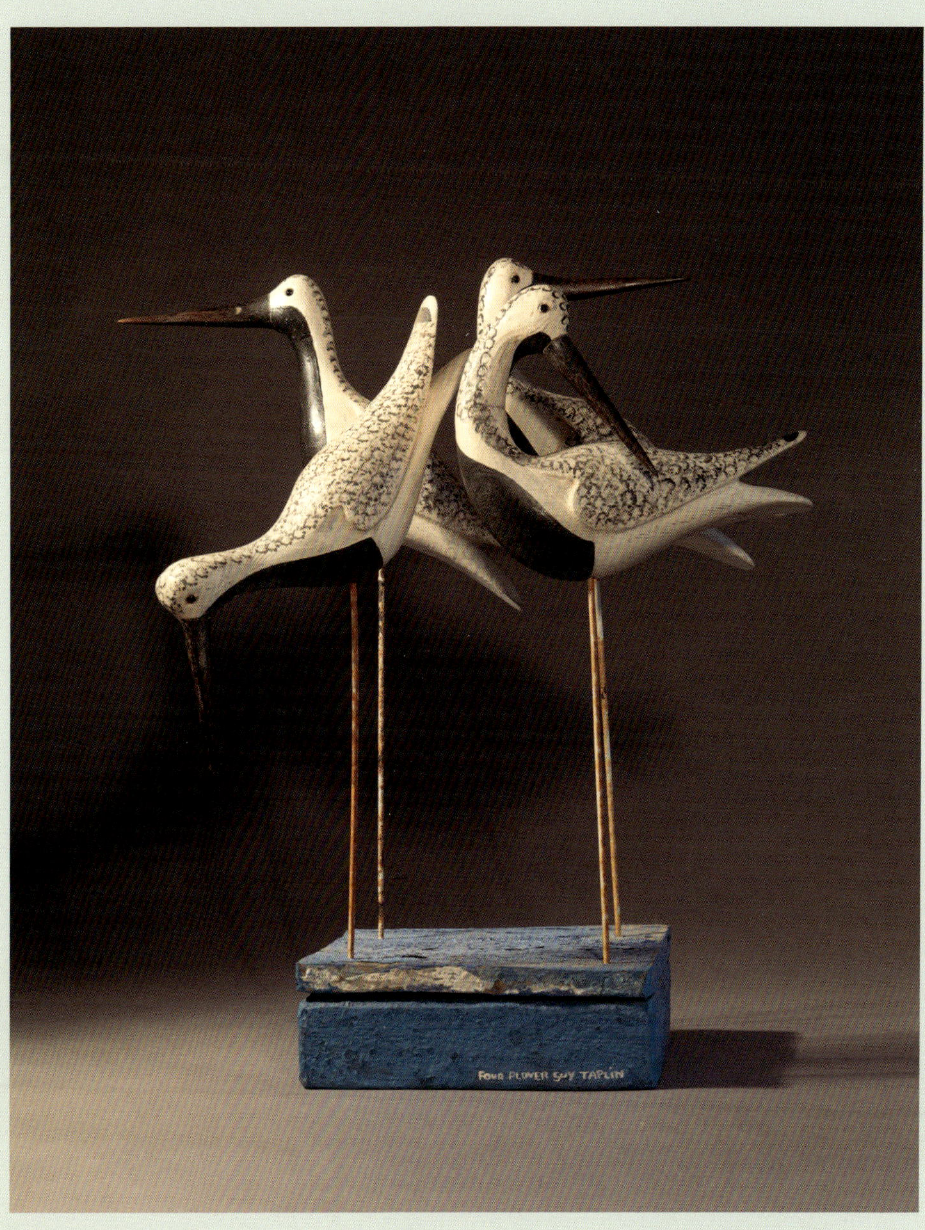

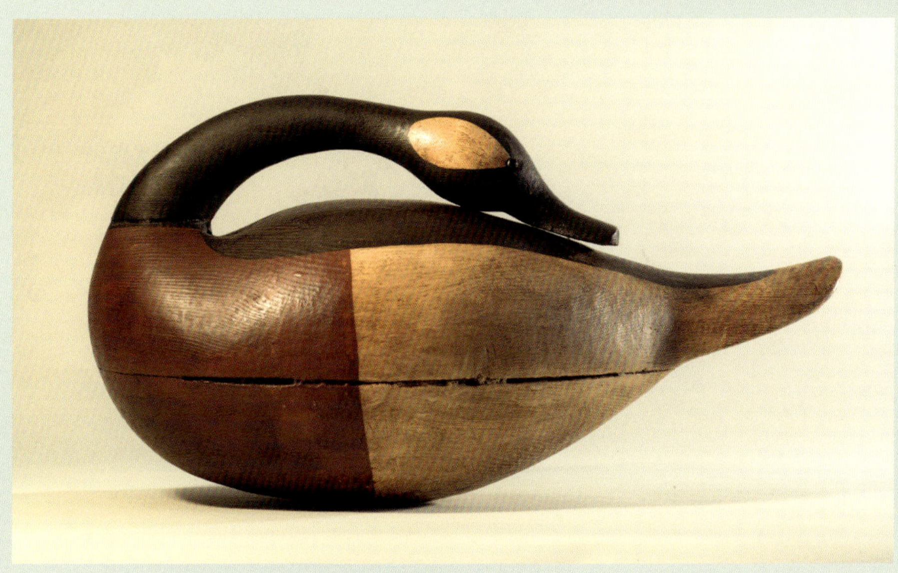

40. **PREENING CANADA GOOSE**
carved and painted driftwood
26 x 50 x 29 cms 10¼ x 19⅝ x 11⅜ ins

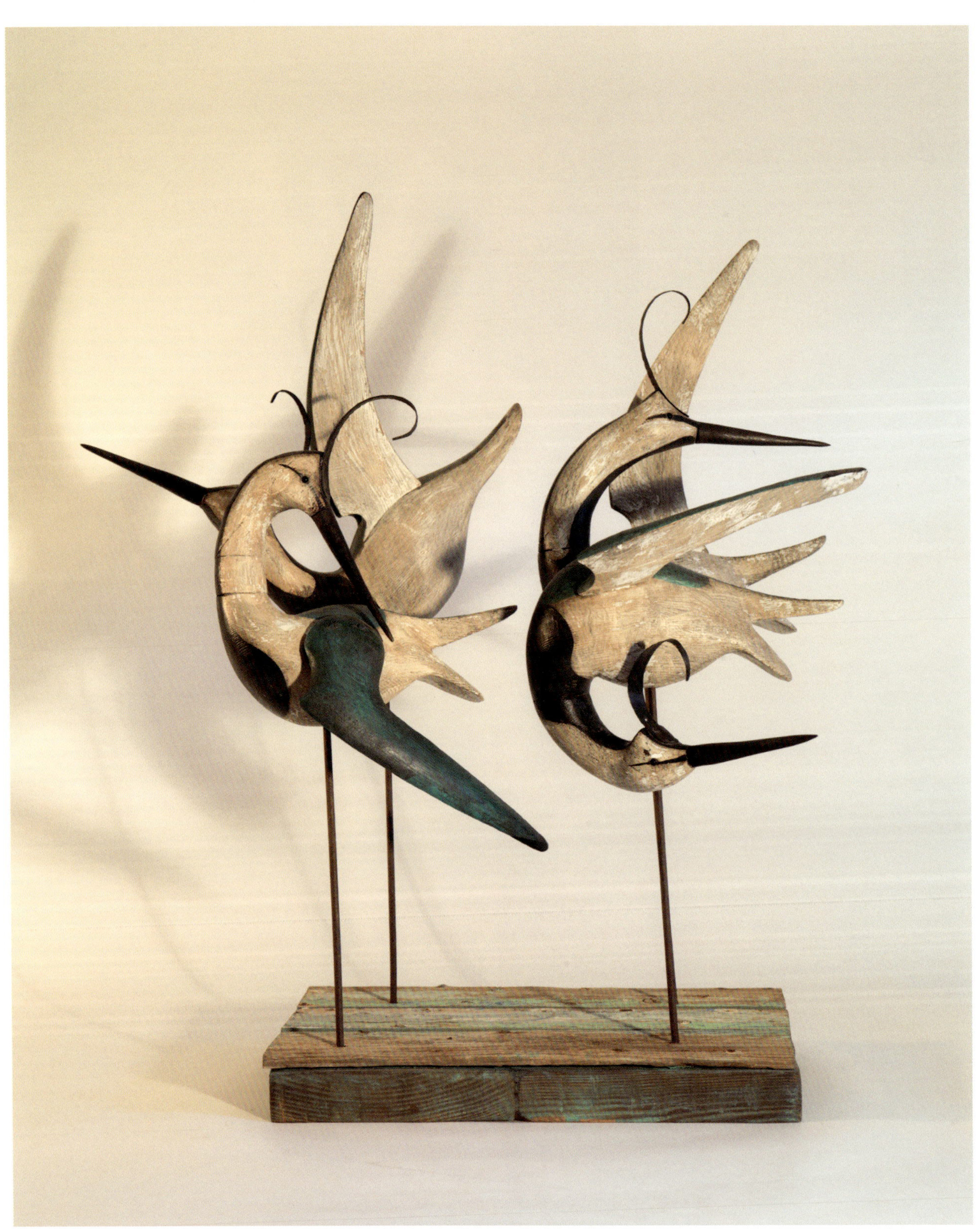

41. FOUR LAPWINGS
carved and painted driftwood
74 x 66 x 41 cms   29⅛ x 26 x 16⅛ ins

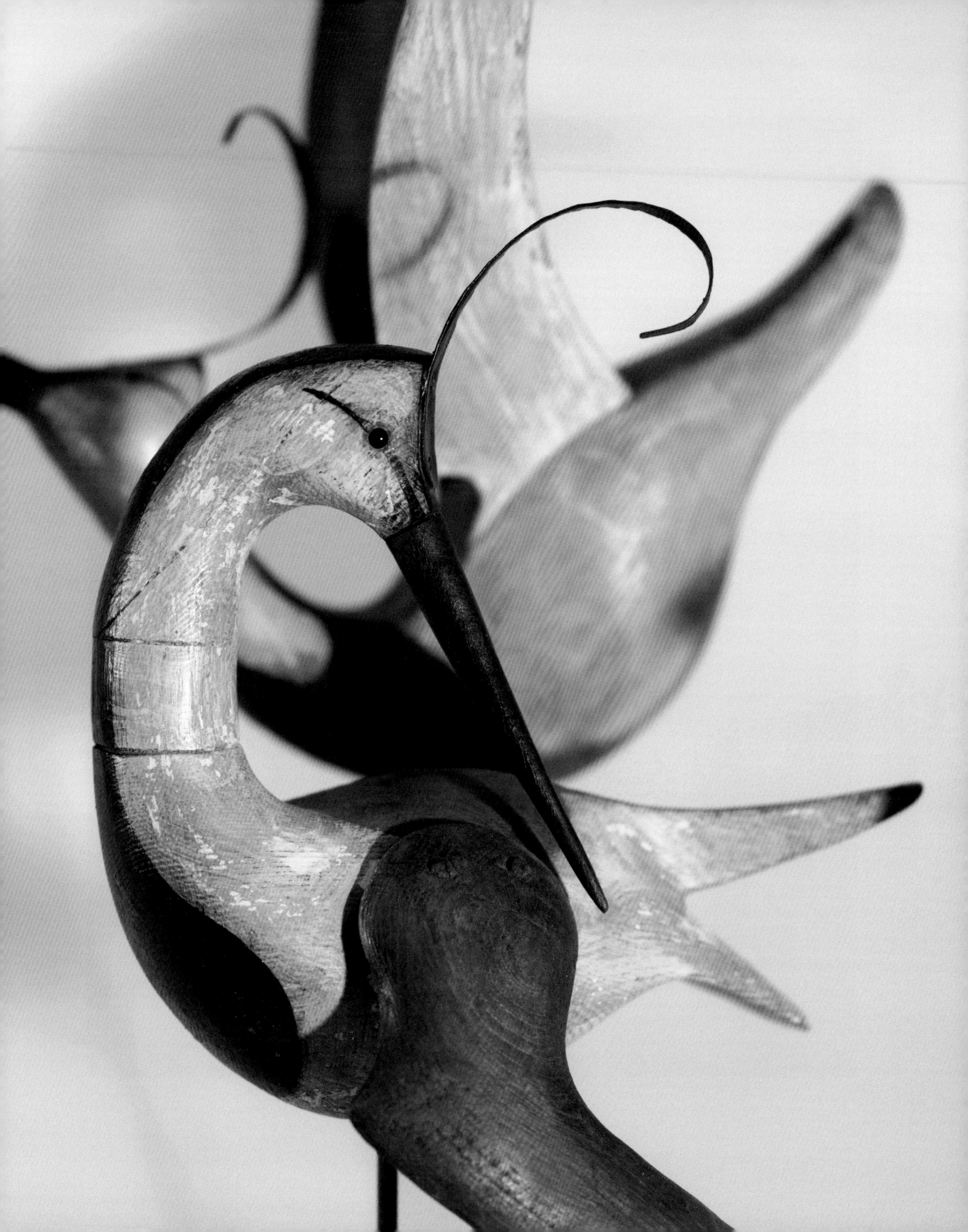

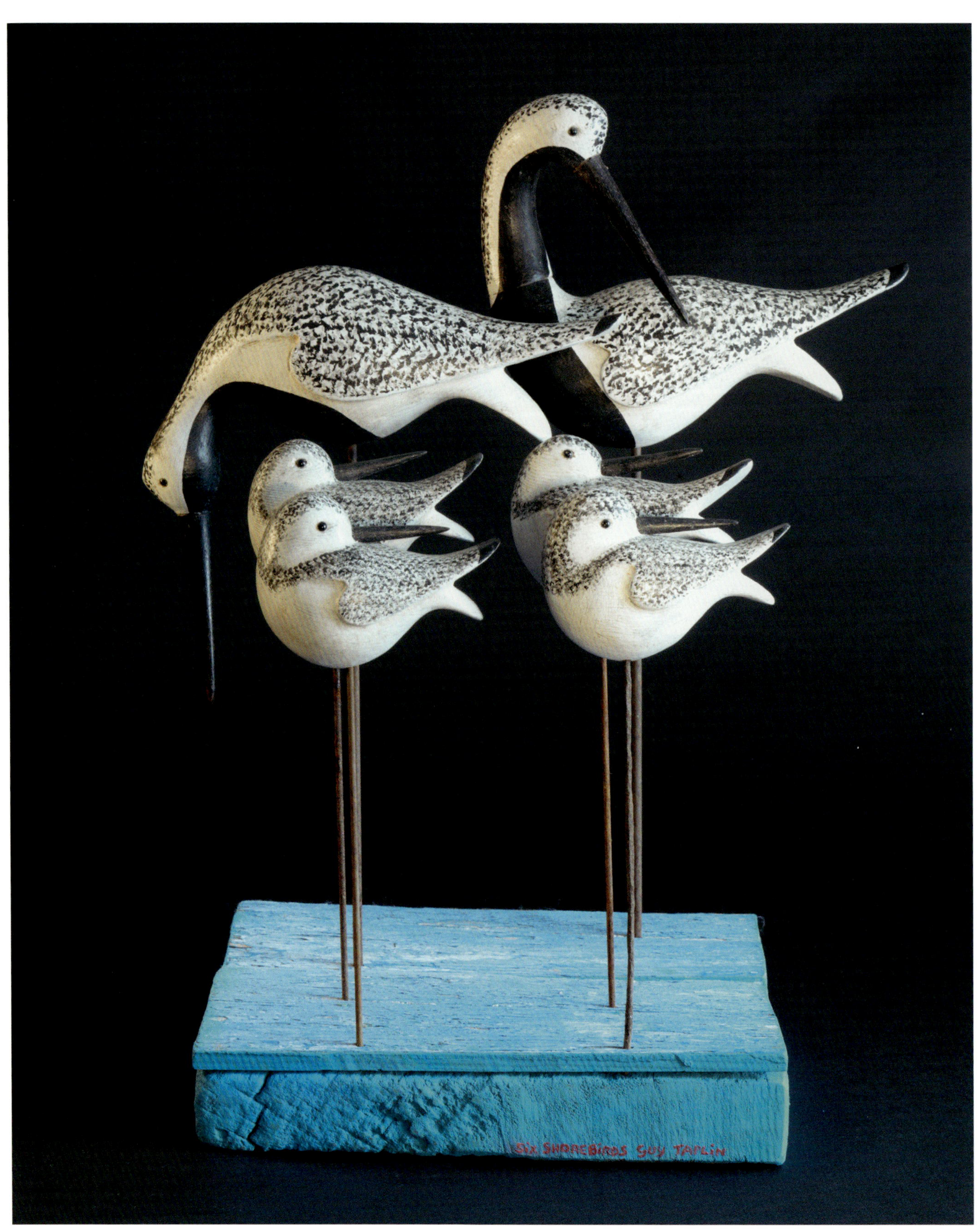

42. **Six Shorebirds**
carved and painted driftwood
60 x 50 x 37 cms   23⅝ x 19⅝ x 14⅝ ins

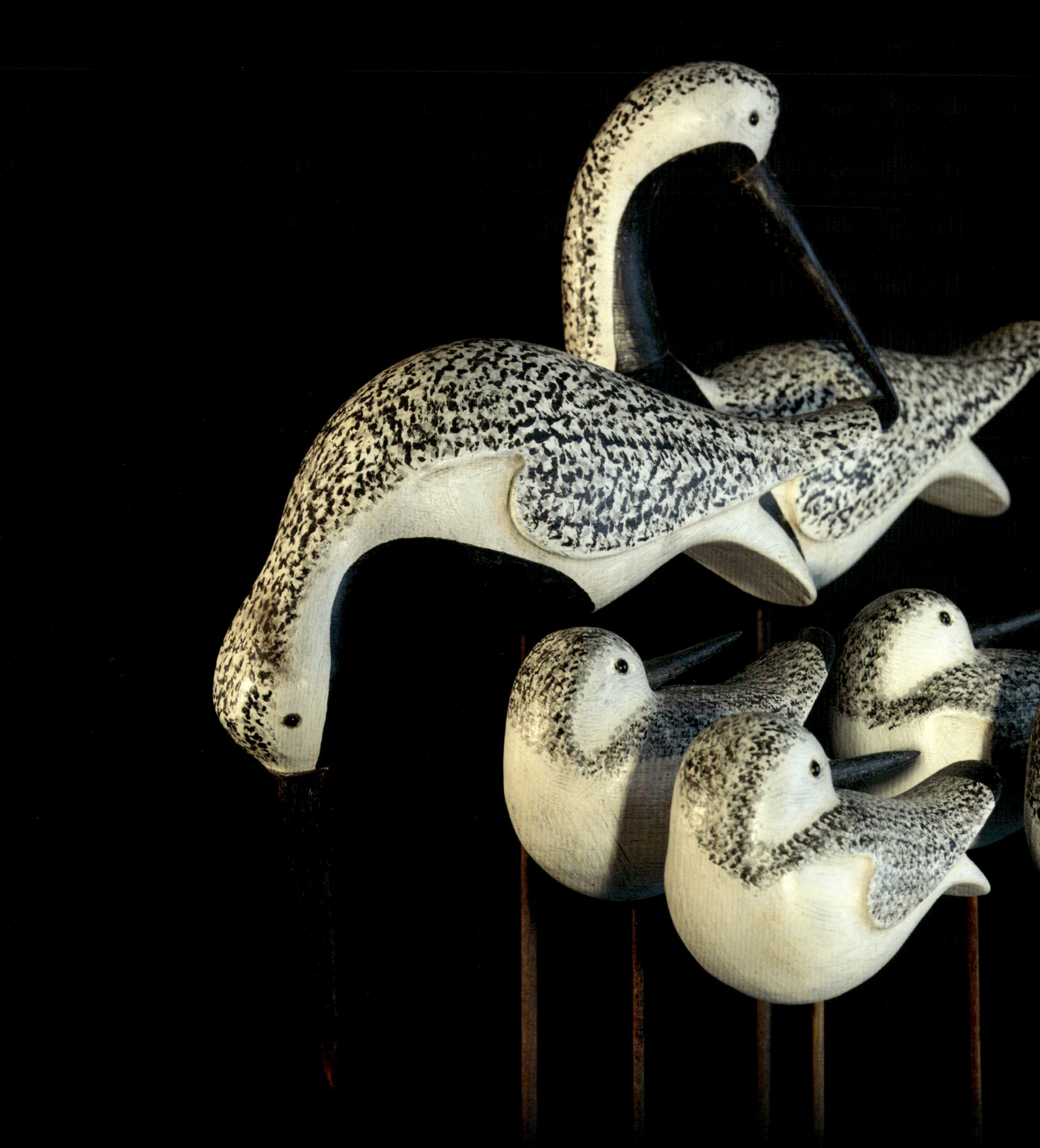

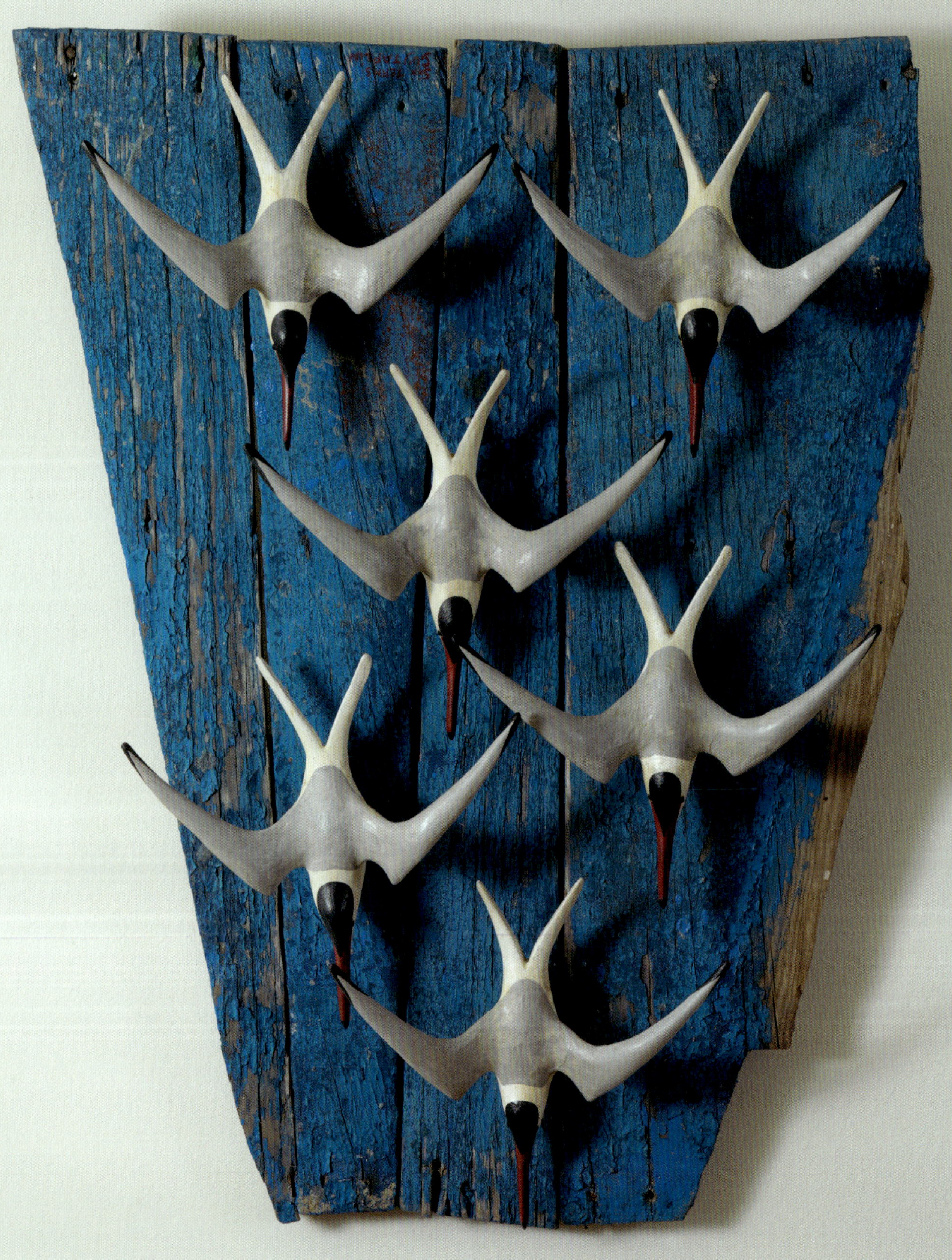

43. Six Flying Terns on a Panel
carved and painted driftwood
69 x 53 x 15 cms 27⅛ x 20⅞ x 5⅞ ins

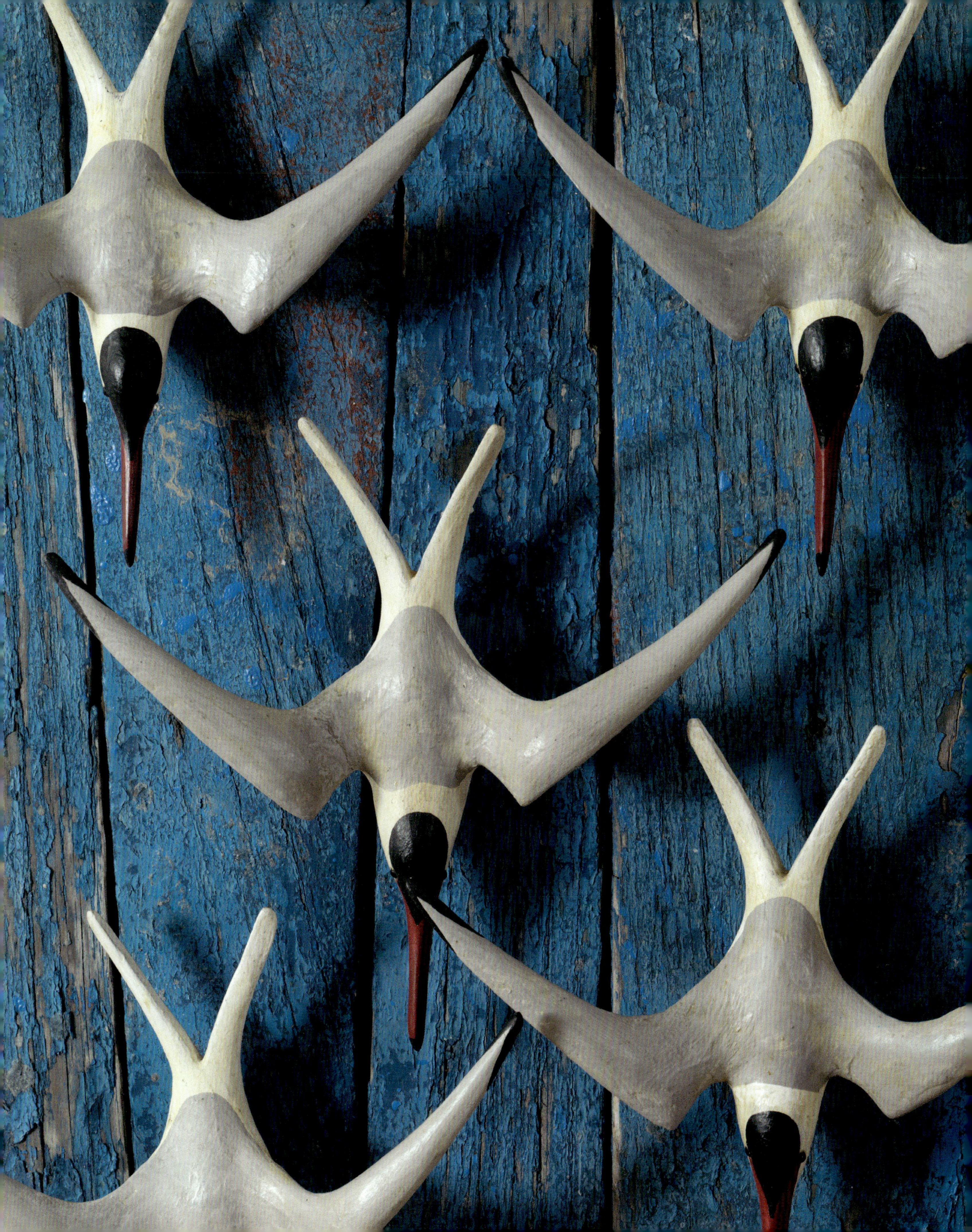

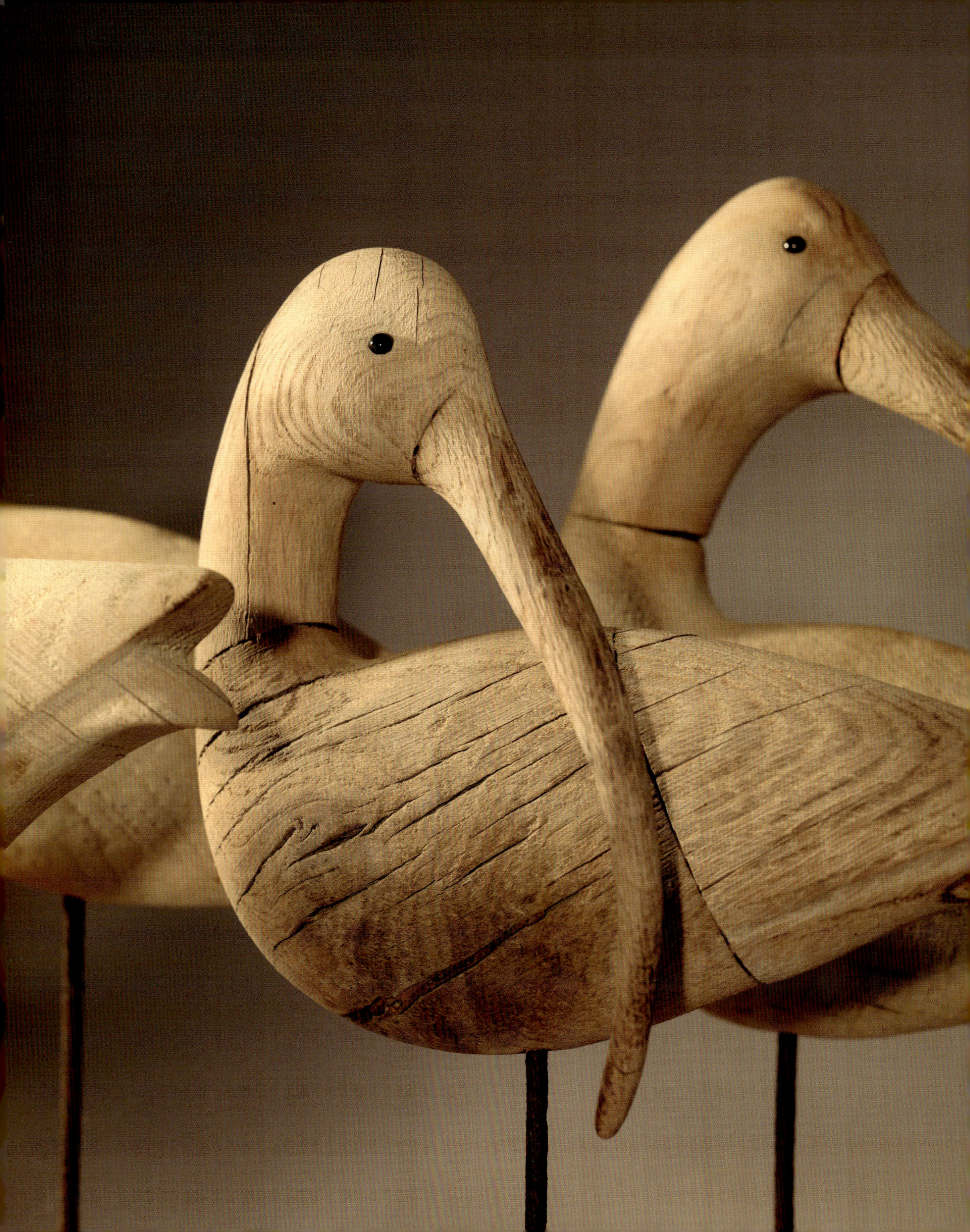

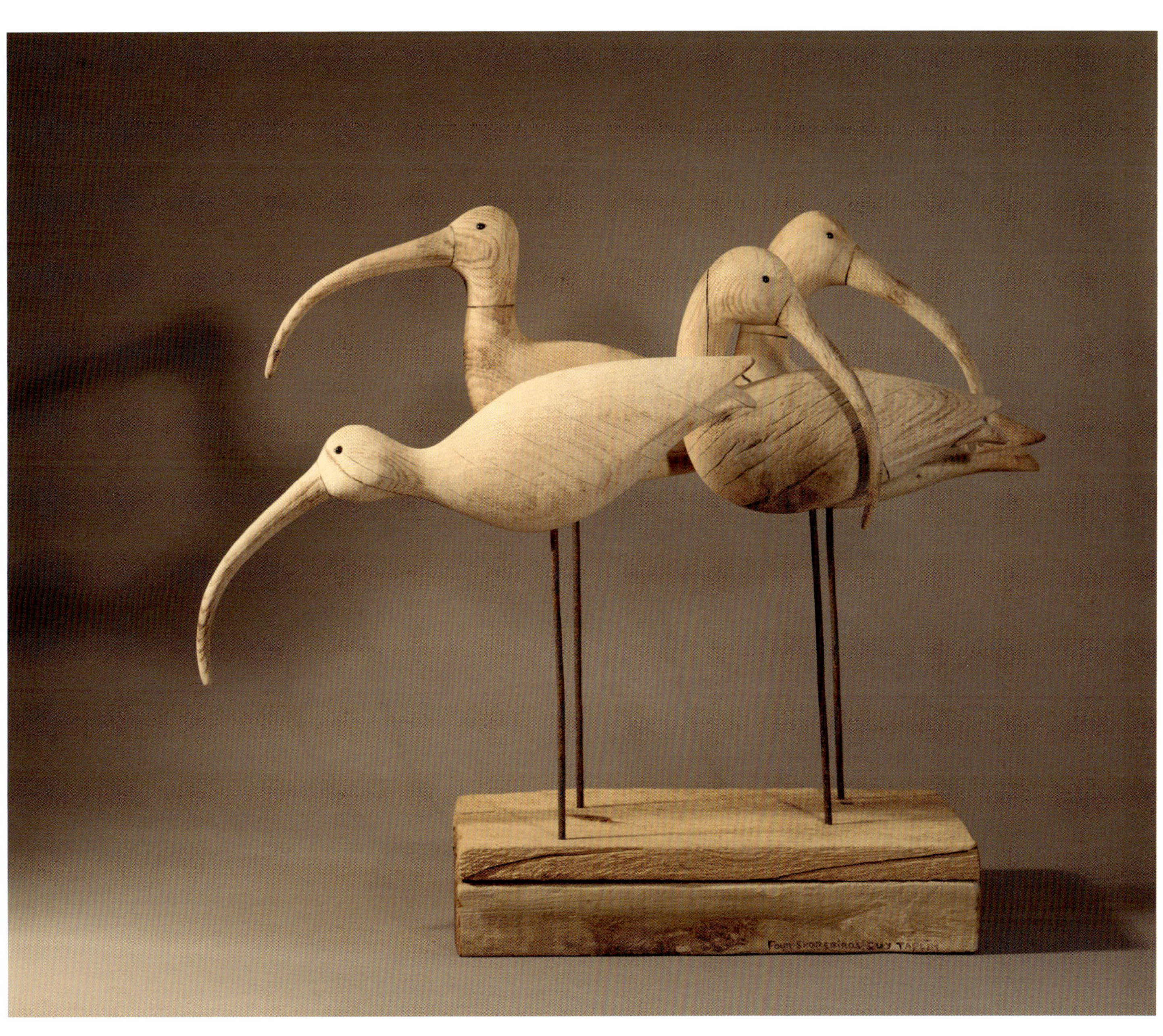

44. Four Shorebirds
carved and painted driftwood
50 x 61 x 25 cms 19⅝ x 24 x 9⅞ ins

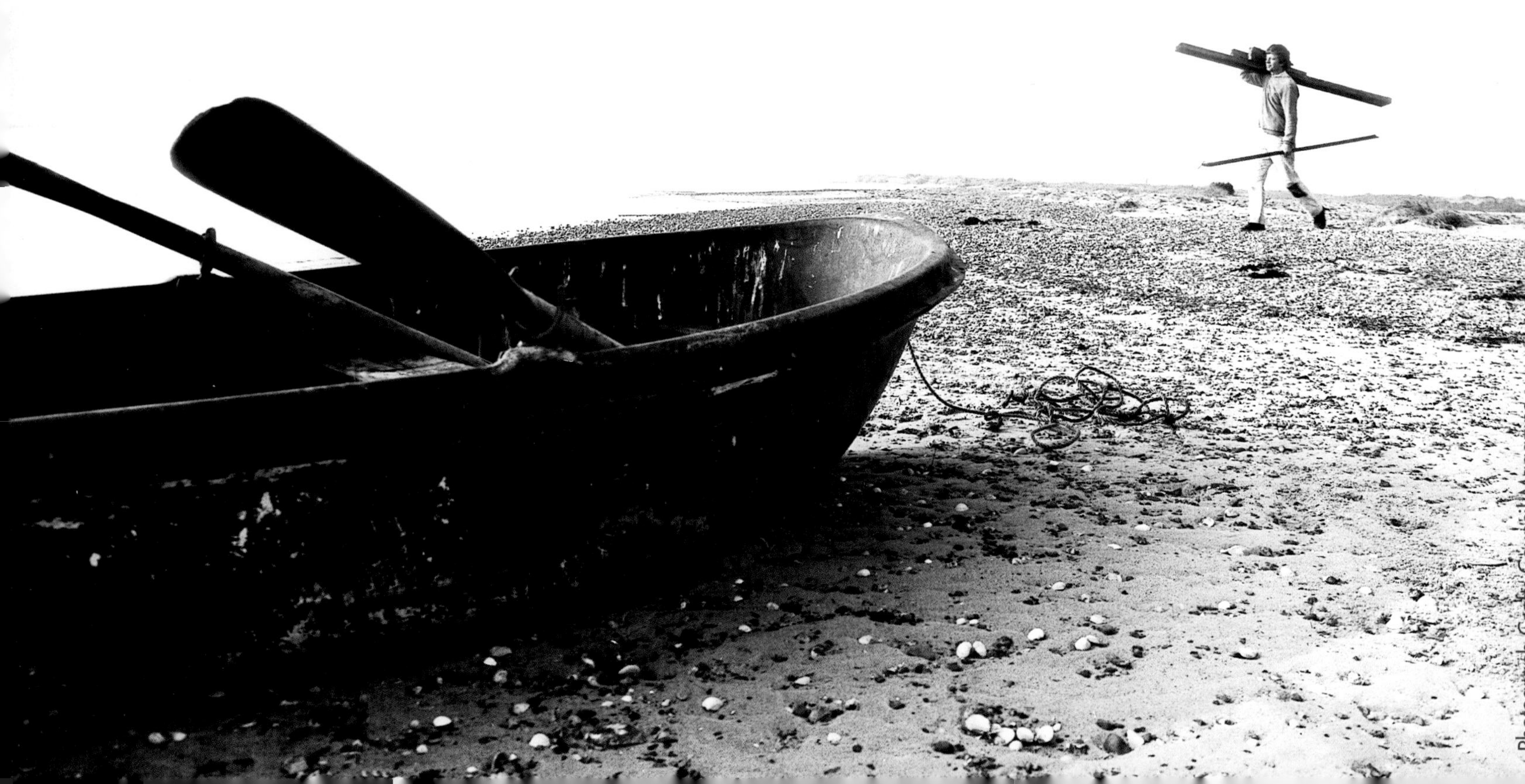

Photograph Crafts Council Magazine

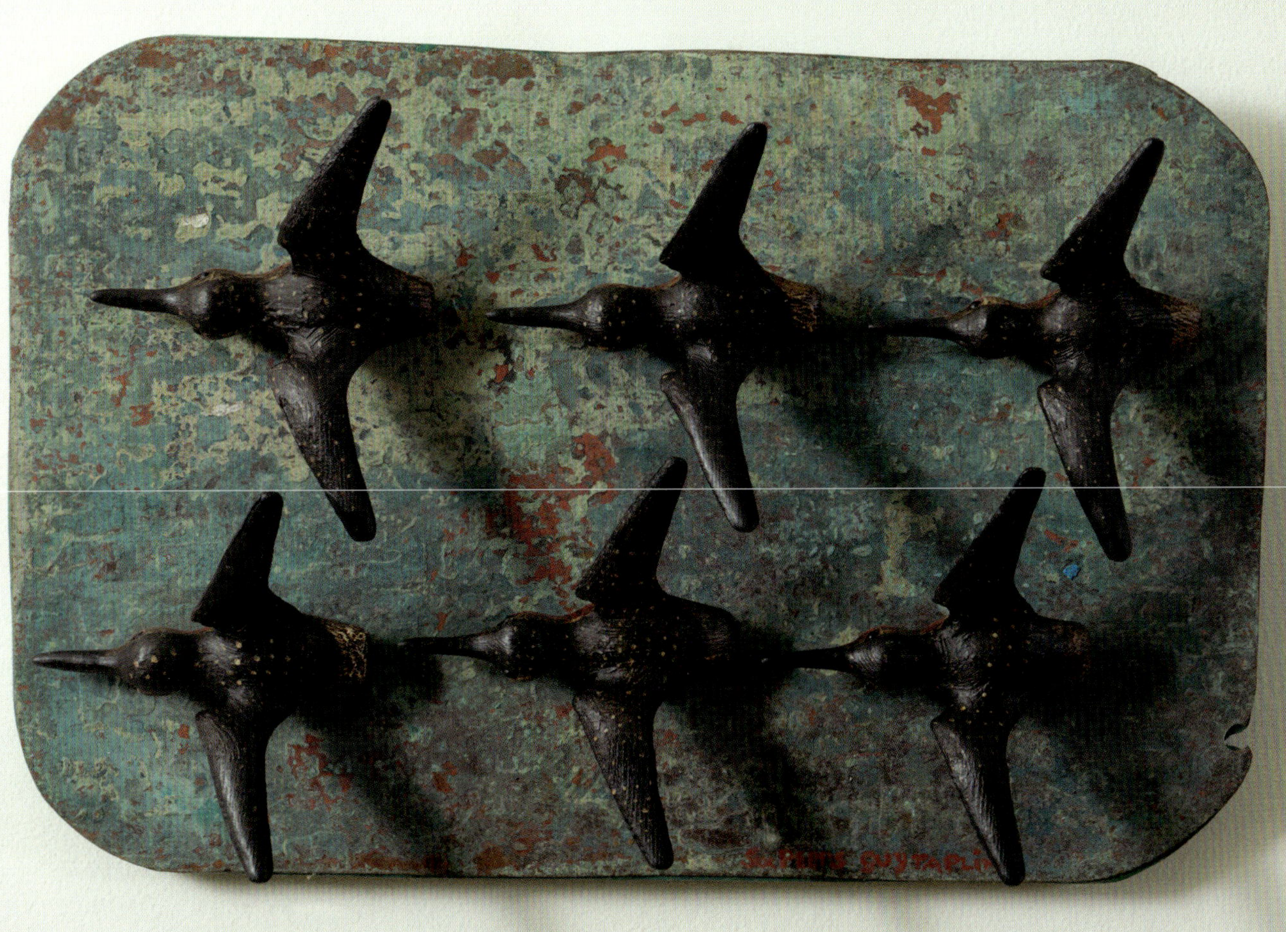

45. **Six Peeps**
carved and painted driftwood
26 x 40 x 9 cms 10¼ x 15¾ x 3⅜ ins

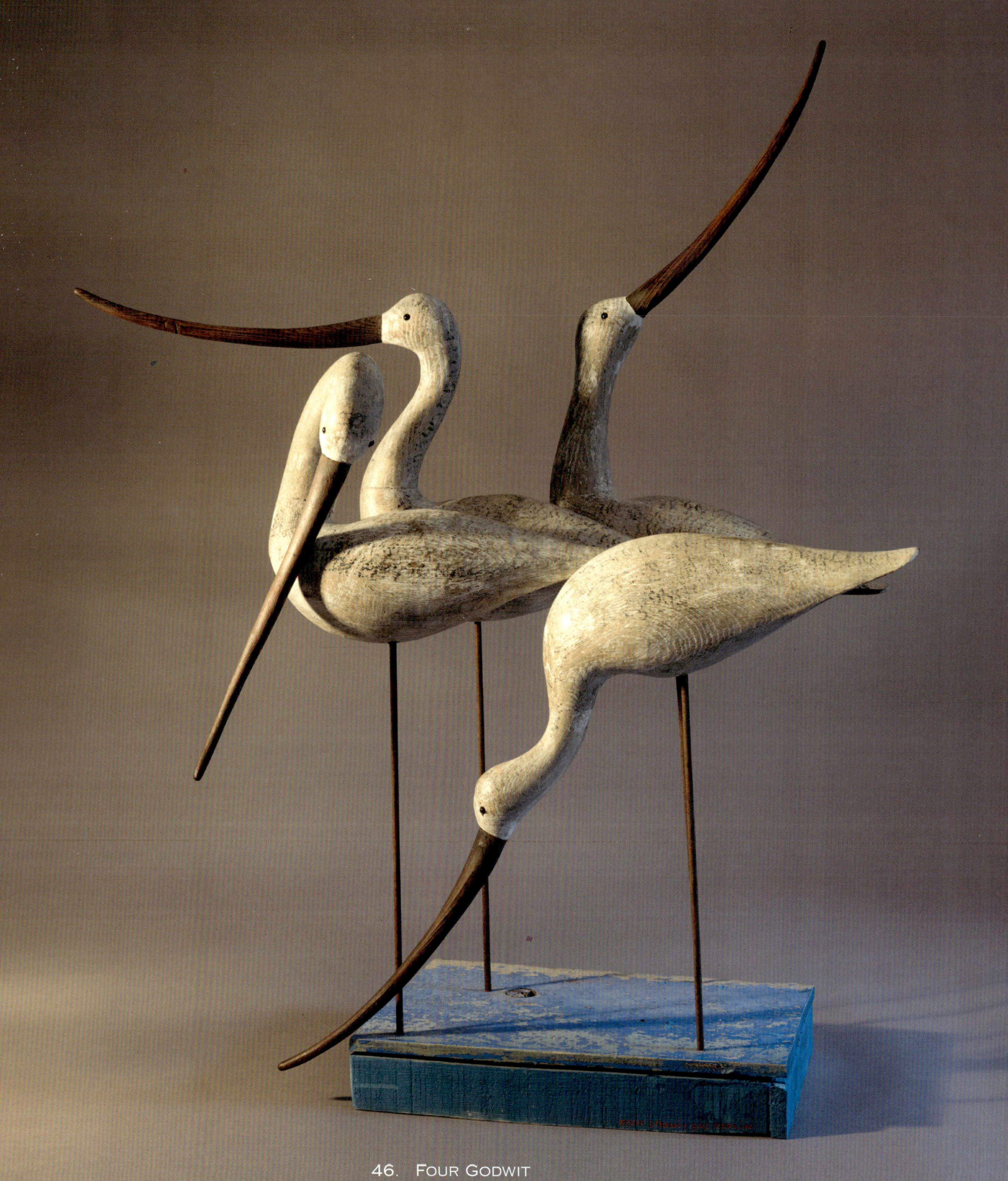

46. FOUR GODWIT
carved and painted driftwood
92 x 76 x 41 cms 36 x 29⅞ x 16⅛ ins

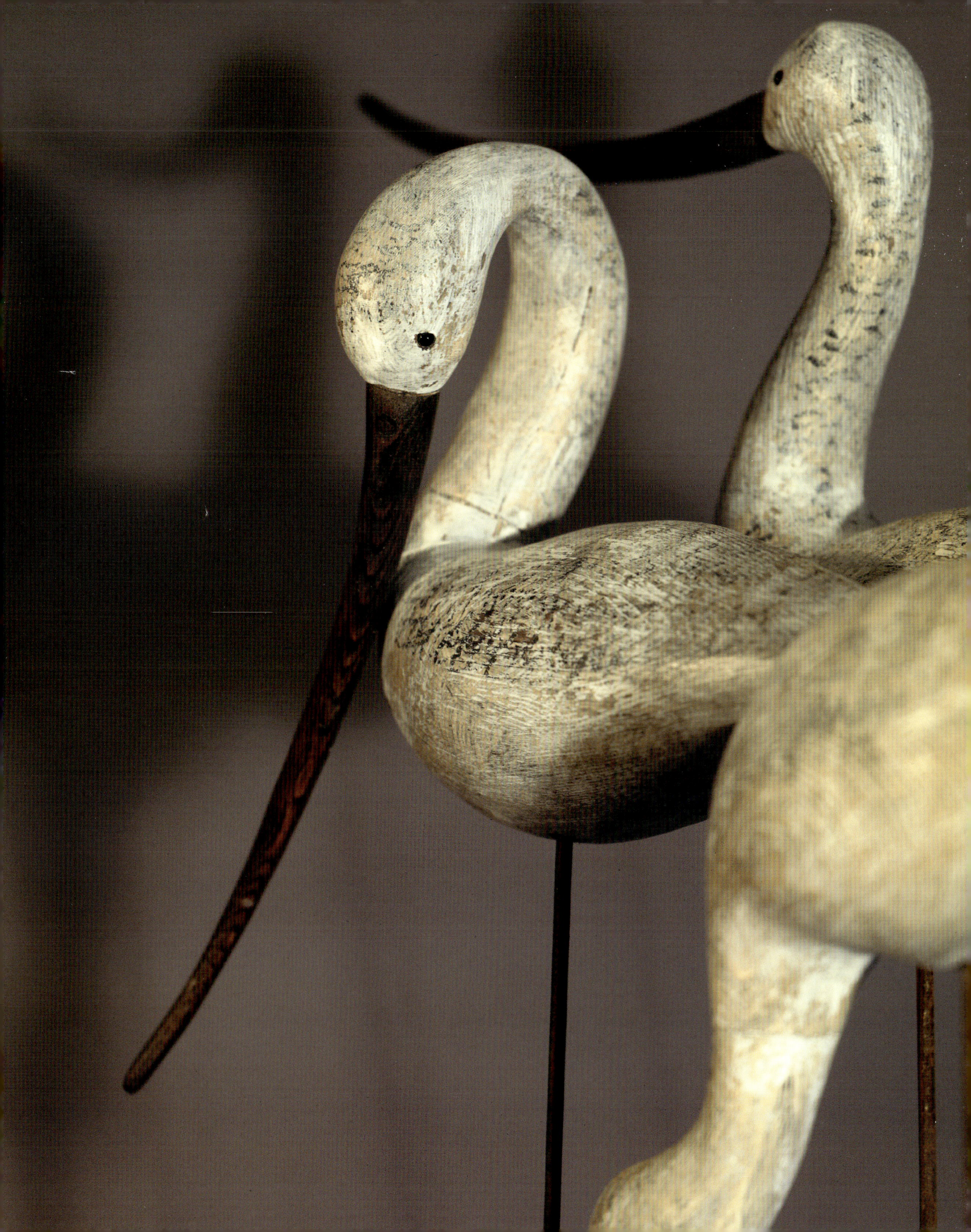

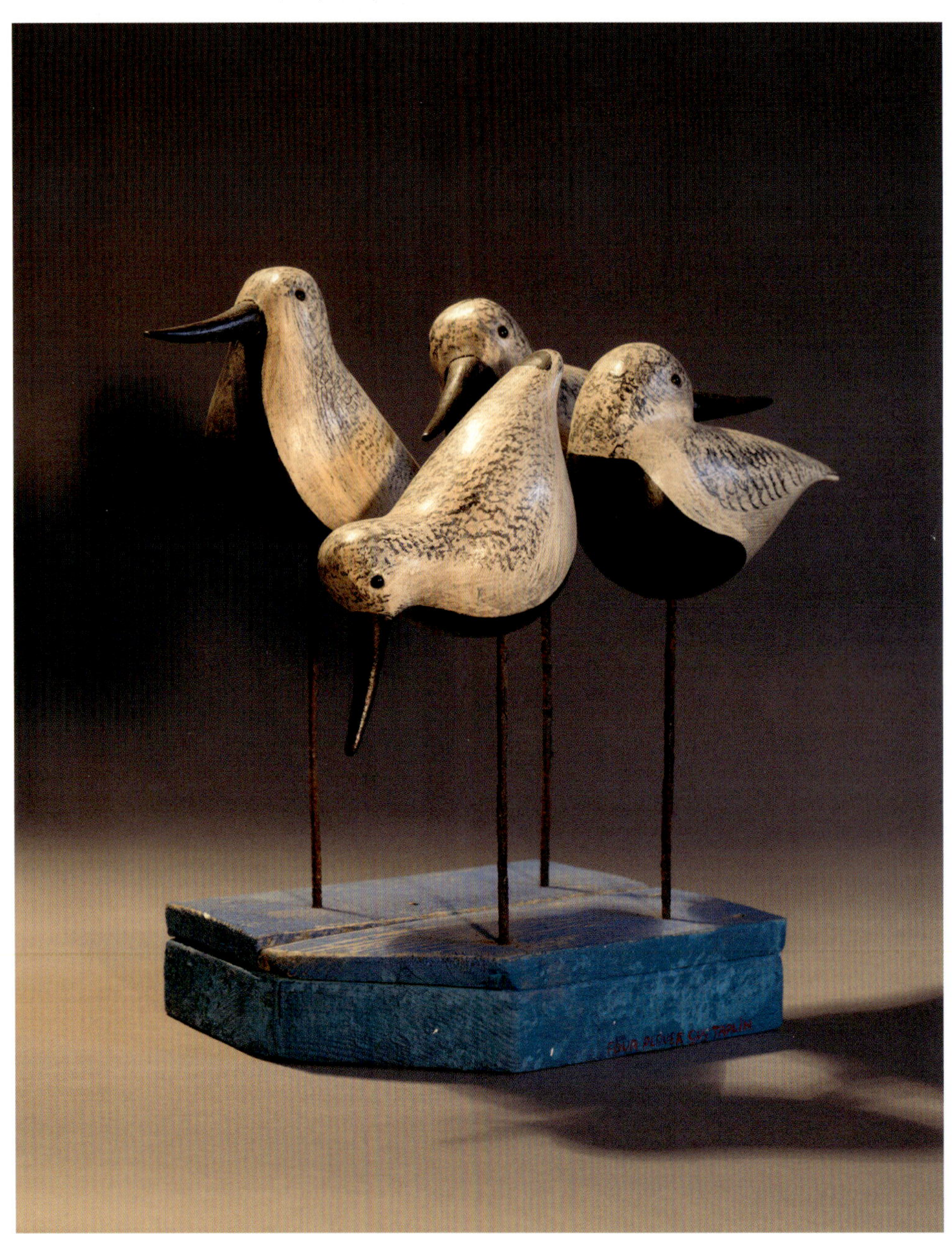

47. **Four Plover**
carved and painted driftwood
34 x 32 x 21 cms 13¼ x 12⅝ x 8¼ ins

48. **Six Redshank** (opposite)
carved and painted driftwood
60 x 71 x 26 cms 23⅝ x 28 x 10¼ ins

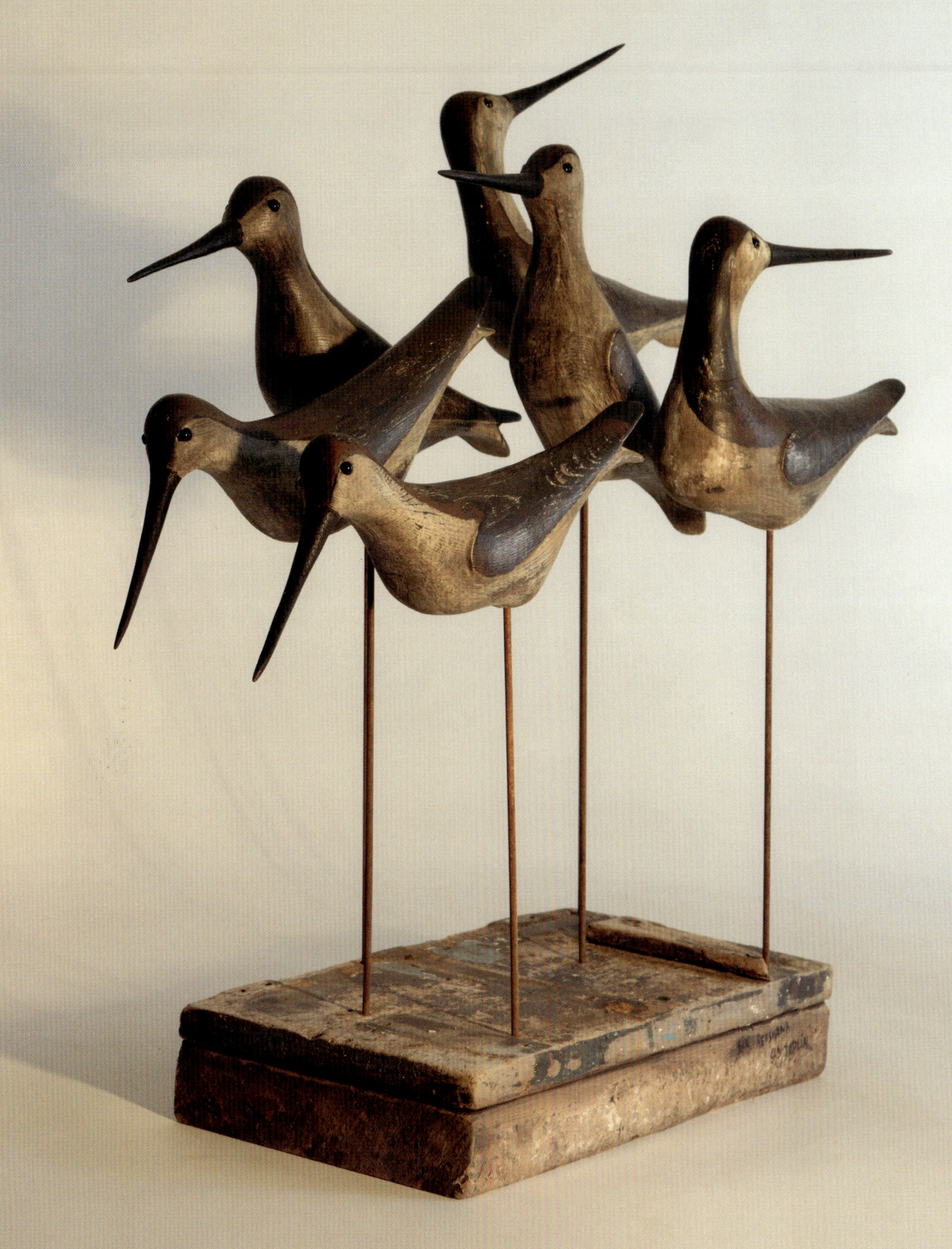

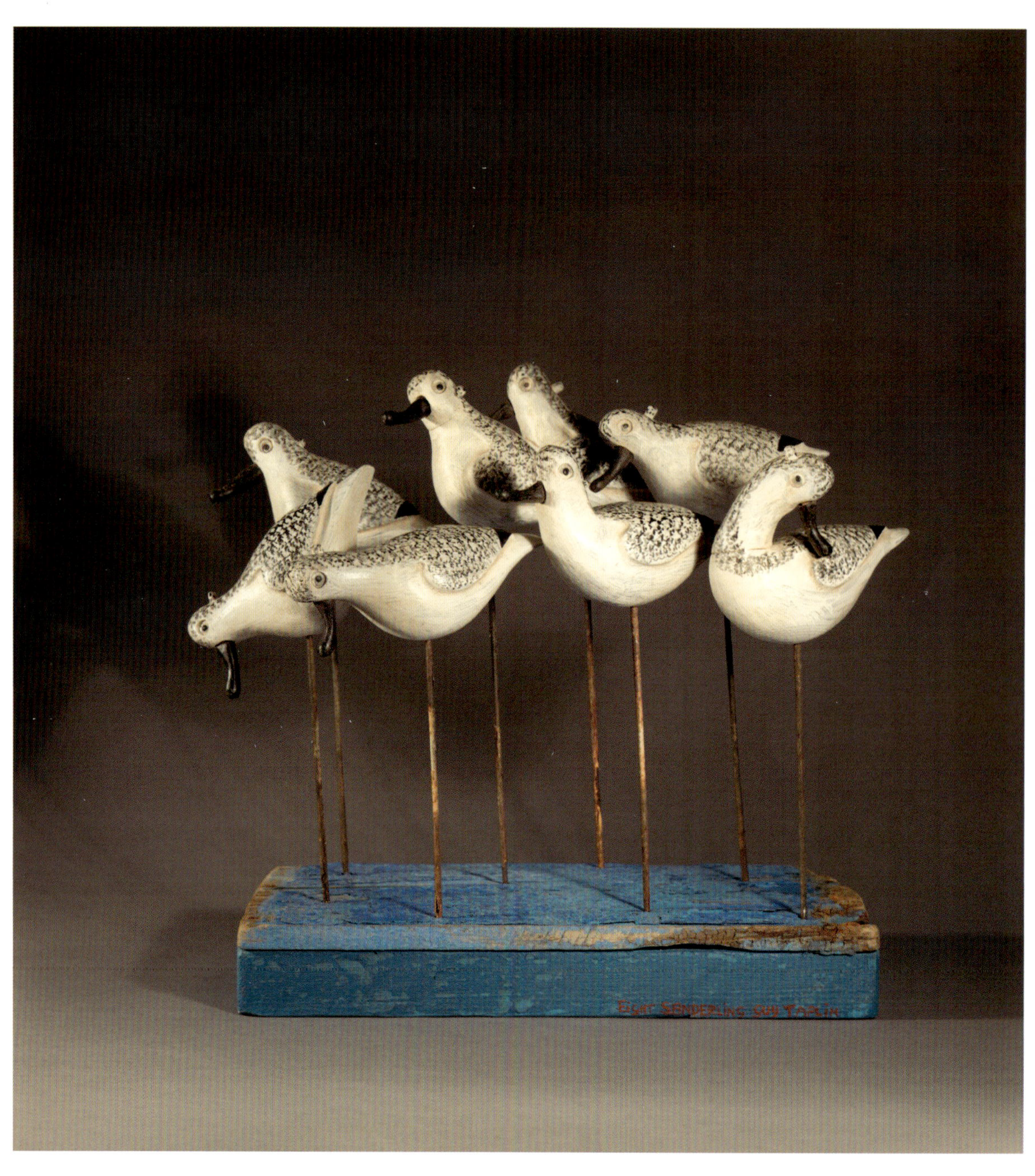

49. **EIGHT SANDERLINGS**
carved and painted driftwood
36 x 43 x 27 cms   14⅛ x 16⅞ x 10⅝ ins

50. **SIX SHOREBIRDS** (opposite)
carved and painted driftwood
44 x 49 x 23 cms   17⅜ x 19¼ x 9 ins

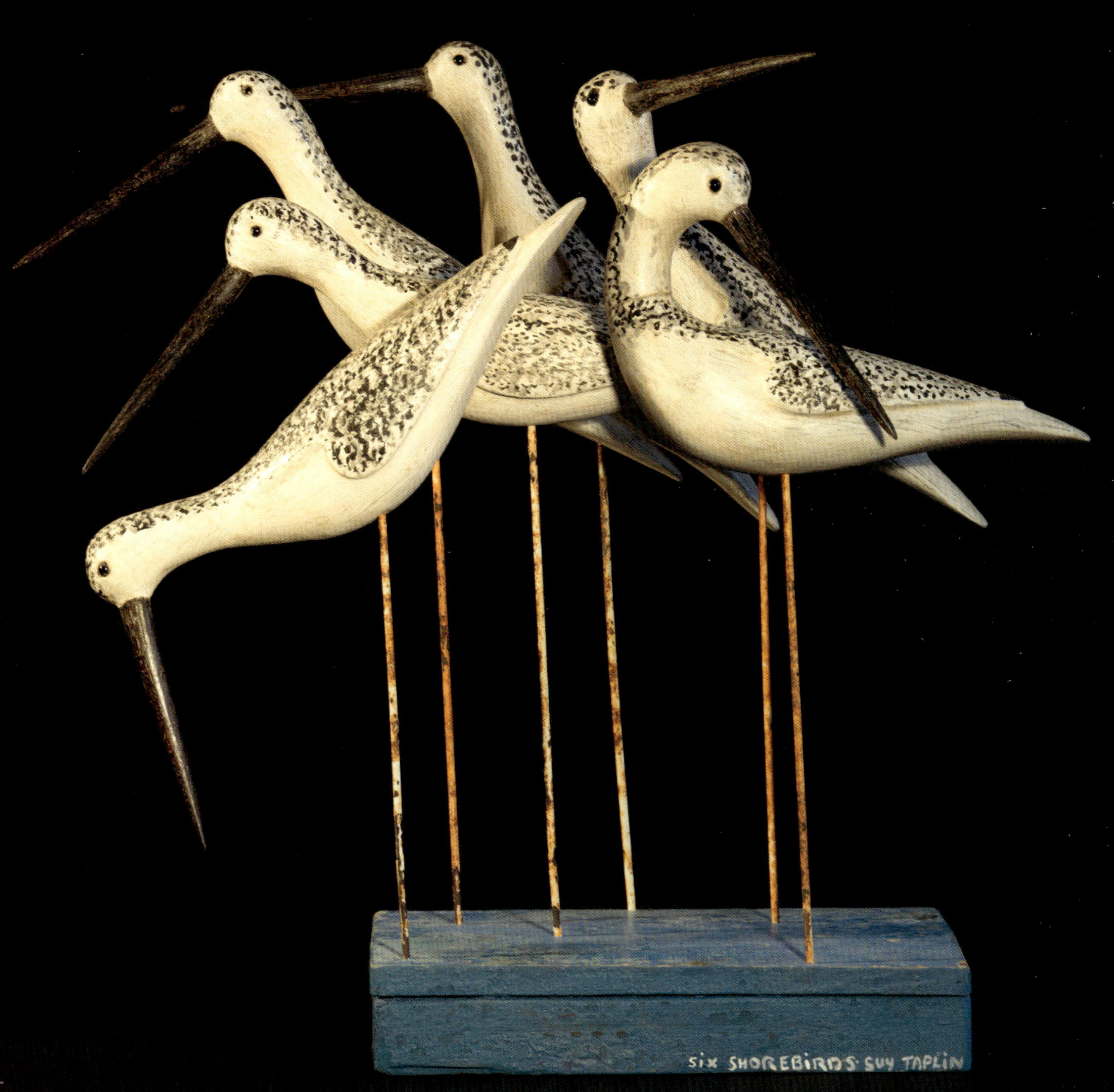
SIX SHOREBIRDS · GUY TAPLIN

GUY TAPLIN

Biography

1939	Born Whitechapel, London, March 5.
1941	Moved to Hereford, where his father worked in a munitions factory, returning to London shortly before the end of the war.
1944	A passion for birds began with the discovery of a nest in a Herefordshire hedgerow, later developed during a city child's egg-collecting expeditions to Epping Forest and elsewhere.
1953	Joined the Post Office as a messenger boy.
1958	Sacked as a GPO cashier after a practical joke in Great Portland Street went awry (stamps worth £2000 got drenched).
1958–60	National Service, including a faked nervous breakdown in Cyprus and a spell in the Netley Psychiatric Hospital in Hampshire. Saw his first artistic posting as a sign painter.
1960–66	Worked as a brewery labourer, hairdresser, window cleaner, lorry driver, television deliverer, seat-belt fitter, lido lifeguard, flypitcher and market trader.
1966	Began a long apprenticeship in Zen Buddhism during which he visited Japan and contemplated becoming a monk.
1967–73	Big-buckled Taplin belts proved popular Flower Power fashion accessories in London, America and Japan. Later decorative designs included tables with brass palm tree supports.
1974	Turned down a job as manager of a Sloane Street fashion business. Became a municipal gardener.
1975-9	Started to whittle in wood decoy-like models of ducks and geese when working as the Bird Man of Regent's Park.
1978	Bought bolt-hole house on the Essex coast. First one-man show, at the Portal Gallery, London; every exhibit is sold.
1979	Married the stained-glass artist Robina Jack. Set up as a bird sculptor with a warehouse studio first on Butler's Wharf and then at Rotherhithe.
1980	Moved permanently to Wivenhoe, near Colchester. Showed in more and more solo and group shows across the United Kingdom and continental Europe (around 100 over the next two decades).
1985	Acquired a studio on the coastal marshes, at the head of the Colne and Blackwater estuaries.
1992	First Taplin birds cast in bronze at the Pangolin Foundry in Gloucestershire.
2001	First solo show with David Messum Fine Art, Cork Street.
2002	Courcoux Contemporary Art Ltd.
2004	Courcoux Contemporary Art Ltd.
2005	Messum's, Cork Street.
2006	Messum's, Cork Street.
2007	Messum's, Cork Street.
2008	Courcoux Contemporary Art Ltd.
2009	Messum's, Cork Street.
2010	Courcoux & Courcoux, *Guy Taplin 25 Knot Out.*
2010	Courcoux & Courcoux, *A Family Affair.*
2011	Messum's, Cork Street.
2012	Courcoux & Courcoux, *Sweet 16.*
2013	Ruthin Gallery, North Wales.
2013	Messum's, Cork Street.
2014	Messum's, Cork Street.
2015	Messum's, Cork Street.

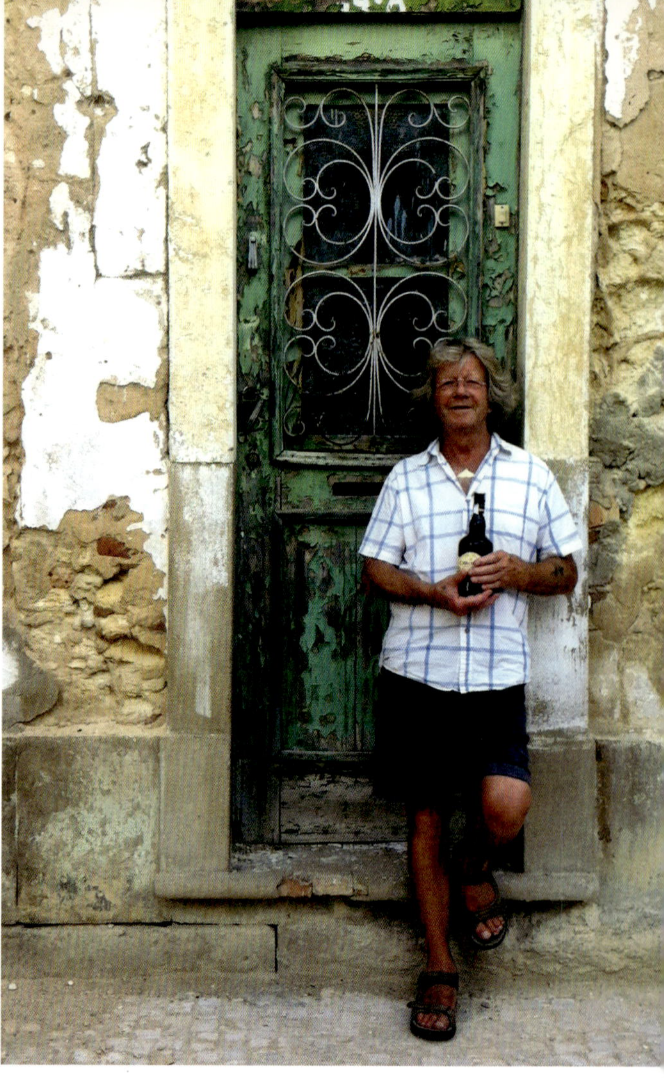

Public collections include:

Tate Gallery
Arts Council of Great Britain
Contemporary Art Society
London Zoo
Royal Bank of Scotland
National Gallery of Modern Art, Edinburgh
Society of Wildlife Artists
Washington State University
Museum fur Kunst und Gewerbe, Hamburg
Anthony Petullo Collection of Self-Taught and Outsider Art, Milwaukee

Private collections include:

Royal Collection; Lady Lavinia Bolton; Uri Geller; Guinness family; Michael Heseltine; Sir Timothy and Lady Hoare; Baroness Kingsmill CBE; Mark Knopfler; David Lean; Joanna Lumley; Lord McAlpine; The Earl of Medway; Mike Nichols; Michael Palin; Sian Phillips; Lord (David) Puttnam; Sainsbury family; Ridley Scott; Jon Snow; Richard Stilgoe; Una Stubbs; Sir Cive Woodward; The late Gerald Durrell; The late Dame Elisabeth Frink; The late Robert Mitchum; The late Jean Muir; The late Jacqueline Onassis; The late Squadron Leader Peter Townsend